Disaster or Culture?

Disaster or Culture?

The Aesthetics Principle and Social Progress

Eckhard Schindler

Translated from the German
by Julia Cooper

Books on Demand

This paperback edition published in 2015 by
BoD – Books on Demand, Norderstedt

Originally published in Germany as *Desaster oder Kultur? Das Ästhetik-Prinzip und der gesellschaftliche Fortschritt* by BoD – Books on Demand, Norderstedt, 2013, 2014.

German National Library Cataloguing in Publication Data:
A catalogue record for this book is available from the German National Library.

ISBN: 978-3-7347-9545-9

Contents

Preface

It would be wonderful to live a life which is characterised by prosperity, appreciation, security, health and domestic happiness, where it is possible to indulge in hobbies and to travel throughout the world, to live in an environment where the dominant attitudes are openness, fairness, compassion and humour, and where one of the biggest irritations is caused by the requirement to make a tax declaration. What else would one want? Then everything would be all right with the world!

Really?

No, there are some details which could disturb the harmony.

There is poverty, crime, environmental devastation. There is the fact that the world is full of escalating conflicts, incongruities, irreconcilabilities, walls and trenches which human beings build against each other with considerable and also completely useless engagement. There is the peculiarity that professional knowledge and technological equipment are developing rapidly, while the competences to manage society systematically and fairly are tending to stagnate disastrously. There is the superficial kind of communication in the media, where catchy statements and lexical know-how counts for more than the more complex interdependencies that would appear if attention were to be less negligent. There is the whole mess, the deep swamp in which we would find ourselves again, if we only dared to open our eyes a bit more.

On closer inspection, it can hardly be denied that human culture is on a very disastrous course. This book will ask the question of whether this is a kind of fateful development, or whether society might be able to prevent the negative trends and find solutions which might be beneficial.

In the first chapter, a few of mankind's problems are summarised under the heading "Culture or disaster?".

Subsequently a few principles and interrelationships are reviewed, which could be helpful in analysing the deficits, or in describing problem-solving approaches. The chapter "The neural system", is initially about the human individual, and the following chapter is about human society and the "mankind organism". Some of the hypotheses presented in these chapters are obtained from the knowledge base of neurology, psychology and philosophy, others are presented as being more or less audacious but as definitely imposing assertions.

The two final chapters (4 and 5) try to provide approaches to solving the problem. On the one hand, this is done by examining mankind's problems, presented in the first chapter, in the light of assumptions from Chapters 2 and 3, and on the other by specifying a few demands or objectives, the fulfilment of which must be made a high priority in order to be able to avert the disastrous way in which development is progressing. As a large part of society's current problems are related to the organisation of the market economy, the penultimate chapter is devoted to a criticism of capitalism. The fifth and final chapter examines the remaining human problems from Chapter 1, and in conclusion it tries to answer the question of how disaster can be averted and how the cultural society can be successfully developed. However, simple or comfortable solutions cannot be presented here.

In particular in the chapters on the neural system (2) and the mankind organism (3), new concepts are introduced at certain points, or employed beyond the normal use of language. This is essential, as this is the only way to adequately highlight the relevant assumptions and arguments, free from the stigma of common conceptual meanings. These deviations are summarised in a glossary at the end of the book.

1 Culture or disaster?

1.1 Environmental devastation and waste of resources

Gigantic amounts of nuclear waste are accumulated, for which there is no solution for either storage or disposal, and for which there may also be no solution in the foreseeable future. Operating nuclear power plants with a residual risk, for which it has long been obvious that this occasionally occurs, is considered to be acceptable. The not insignificant risk of radioactive contamination of larger or smaller areas is accepted.

Large amounts of CO2 are pumped into the atmosphere by using fossil fuels. The global increase in temperatures that this causes will, in all probability, accelerate through methane, which escapes from the permafrost soil of vast regions. The idea of depositing CO2 under the earth's surface tends to be more like a bounced cheque than that of a solution. The rise in temperatures and sea levels caused by human activity is inevitable. Climate zones will shift. Where this development will lead is not at all clear. A consensus of the global powers to stop this development, which would be more or less adequate, is not in sight. Today there is already an increase in disasters and famines caused by the accumulation of extreme weather conditions. Islanders in the Pacific are preparing to leave their paradises.

It is regarded as acceptable that overhead power lines, solar parks and wind power plants disfigure the environment, at least by those who do not have to live in the immediate vicinity of a wind farm or an overhead power line. Hydro power plants, regarded as more environmentally-friendly, lay beautiful countryside to waste and sometimes cause enormous landslides and many deaths. To produce gas, large volumes of the rock structure are destroyed deep underground and large amounts of water are polluted by chemicals through the extraction method called fracking, or “hydraulic fracturing”.

Human beings breathe oxygen. At the same time, however, they have such little regard for this gas that they use large amounts of it to feed energy processes which are used for comfort, as well as cars and many other gadgets.

Man’s interventions in his environment continually lead to a significant decimation in biodiversity. Agriculture and livestock farming are practised on such a grand scale that artificially established monocultures replace naturally grown habitats and conventional agricultural methods. The dislocation of species leads to the displacement of endemic species, which could survive for a long time in isolated environments. Some of the species introduced in any environment disperse again in an extreme, unchecked manner, as they no longer come across natural predators or competitors there. With genetic engineering, accidents are accepted without any major scruples, which lead to the displacement of naturally or conventionally grown species by synthetic species. The value of complex natural balances, which have developed over many million years of perpetual evolution, is met with unbelievable ignorance. The ability of the human being to be able to act as a successful bio-designer is excessively overrated, while at the same time the negative consequences are gradually revealed. Quite impressive partial successes are facing the disastrous action of the whole of humanity.

Forests and habitats which are beneficial for the balance between CO_2 and O_2 are falling victim to a drastic process of destruction.

Land and oceans are inexorably enriched with waste. Individual activities and initiatives to prevent and eliminate environmental damage conflict with the general acceptance of the active contamination of the environment and the risk of environmental accidents, motivated by profit-seeking.

It is true that this development and the disastrous actions of human beings are in principle noted – there are countless more or less influential movements which also already result in reversals. However, in this regard one can only characterise human activity as a whole as divided, ambivalent and fatalistic. The capacity for insight and reactions which would really be appropriate to the dimension of this problem is not apparent. Comfortable living conditions, which on closer examination are based on disastrous environmental damage, are as far as possible accepted unconditionally and are expanded. Where, because of social or economic problems, a reduction in comfortable living conditions has to be made, the question of environmental protection becomes even more peripheral. In areas where poverty prevails, environmental protection tends not to be an issue, but normally there is less of a contribution towards causing global ecological crop damage.

The scientific-technical revolution resulted in the discovery of many possibilities on how one can use the earth's resources for a more pleasant way of life. The market-organised consumer society acts as a stimulus to use these possibilities extensively. As part of globalisation, the capitalist-market-based model is exported throughout the world. The mechanisms of this economic system, which largely shapes global developments, build on the basis of constant growth and the constant extensive exploitation of resources.

Fossil fuels, such as coal, oil and natural gas, which have evolved over many aeons through cycles of nature, will be almost completely depleted within a few centuries. They will either be converted into substances that are harmful to life, or converted extremely quickly into natural substances. For raw materials which have retained a high value in terms of prosperity and the market economy, such as precious metals, rare earth elements etc., there is an acceptance of extraction processes that contaminate and devastate whole areas.

It is characteristic of human beings that they mercilessly exploit resources which initially appear to be available in infinite amounts. This already happened in antiquity, for example in the Mediterranean area with the forests. Likewise, today the abundant fish population in the oceans is being depleted. A change of course is often not possible until almost all deposits have been exhausted, so that extraction is no longer profitable.

Complex equilibriums, whose synergies have developed over many millions of years, are being eradicated by human beings in an amateurish way. Using scientific knowledge, which seems to be very progressive but, as measured by the immense wealth of nature, appears to be naive, there is diligent intervention in all accessible systems. The result is a dramatic reduction in the emergence of resources, the progressive destruction of equilibriums, and the decimation of biodiversity.

There is definitely an awareness in society about treating the environment and resources in a considerate way, responsibility for the need for sustainable economic activity is recognised in part, and is fought for. However, overall, from a global perspective, the actions of human beings are disastrous in this regard.

1.2 Population explosion, famine and global resource demand

The global population is growing rapidly.

Two aspects should be noted in this regard:

- The direct link between poverty, population growth and a continuing humanitarian catastrophe.
- The consequences accruing from this for the development of the global population and the increasing demand for resources.

The global famine is summarised by Jean Ziegler (2013, xiii) in the following words:

> "The destruction, every year, of tens of millions of men, women, and children from hunger is the greatest scandal of our era. Every five seconds, a child under the age of ten dies of hunger – on a planet abounding in wealth and rich in natural resources. In its current state, the global agricultural system would in fact, without any difficulty, be capable of feeding 12 billion people, or twice the world's current population. Hunger is thus in no way inevitable. Every child who starves to death is murdered."

However, this is only the tip of the iceberg of humanitarian catastrophe, or rather it is only the most blatant symptom of the global problem of poverty:

> "Since 1975 fifty-eight countries of the South have sunk into poverty. They are home to the *Bottom Bil-*

lion, the one billion people who represent the lowest level of poverty." (Ziegler 2011, 88f.)

The problem of hunger is also particularly exacerbated by the fact that in many poor countries of the world, agricultural areas are strategically bought up, or used directly for the production of biofuels. Frequently, financially strong investors join together with corrupt forces in the countries involved in order to pursue profitable aims. In many cases, families are deprived of the opportunity of continuing to live from the (subsistence) agriculture that is organised for their own needs. In other cases, large amounts of global ecological wealth end up on the sacrificial altar and monocultures are used to replace old-growth forests, for example. (see the chapter "The Vultures of 'Green Gold'" in Ziegler 2013 177ff.).

At the same time, population growth in poorer regions, where having a large number of children is the most important form of security for old age, is particularly extreme. On the one hand, the close relationship between poverty, hunger and dramatic population growth is statistically proven, on the other it is also obvious and generally known. From the daily news we can already conclude that in the poor regions of Asia, sub-Saharan Africa, South America etc. there must be a proportional relationship between the trends mentioned.

The interdependency between poverty and a shortage of resources, scarce agricultural productivity and excessive population growth is a vicious circle which actually belongs in the millennium before last not, however, in our world of scientific progress and the global triumphal march of high technology. The scale of this humanitarian catastrophe is staggering. The negative role accorded to globalisation will be examined in more detail below.

The second aspect, the phenomenal increase in the global population and the demand for resources at global level, has the potential to complete the human disaster. Poverty, as well as the trend towards population growth, prevails not just in the poorest countries in the world but also in the developing countries, emerging nations, as well as in regions with an average level of development. Only in a few predominantly rich countries is the trend towards population growth partly reversed.

However, in parallel to this a gradual trend towards prosperity is taking place in many of the countries concerned. The consequence is that the wasteful handling of globally available resources, which the prosperous consumer society has adopted, is dramatically increasing year by year.

An important fundamental right is the right to a humane existence. On the one hand, it is a travesty that it is not possible to implement this all over the world. On the other hand, that would lead to clearly increased participation in the exchange processes of the affluent society. If one were to extrapolate the behaviour and trends of this society as they are currently presented, the consequence would be an environmental and resource problem on a scale that would be the end of civilisation.

It appears as if humanity neither wants to remove the shame of poverty, nor that it can do so. In any case, there is no solution without a profound shift in values and a profound change in the behaviour of the global population, which certainly does not entitle us to hope that it will ever be achievable.

1.3 Striving for power, violence and wars

The life of all species on planet earth is characterised by the constant fight for resources and living space. Here there is a constant interplay between competition and the struggle for survival, on the one hand, and food chains, symbioses and synergies on the other. The life forms and behavioural patterns which have developed from this seem, on the one hand, to be a wonderfully multifarious variety of flora and fauna. On the other, it is also noticeable that every means – up to brutal force – is allowed to help to assert the interests of one's own species.

The human being, although he is quite a particular kind of mammal, is no exception here, at least from a historical point of view. The characteristics and accomplishments which we can refer to today in relation to humans have clearly not resulted in a view that we have successfully liberated ourselves from the side of the animals.

On the one hand there is culture, art, education, science, humanitarian organisations, global organisations, democratic political systems with constitutions which declare human dignity to be sacrosanct, a "Universal Declaration of Human Rights", of politics characterised by social and ethical motives, political diplomacy, globally functioning flows of information, goods and money and many other miracles of human society.

On the other hand, there is regularly a return to behavioural patterns that seem like those of animals, in which all previously mentioned accomplishments are trampled underfoot. The history of humanity is a history of wars, genocides, regimes murdering their own population. The President of a democratic country (Dwight D. Eisenhower) orders the assassination of a politician (Patrice Lumumba), who represented the only hope for democracy in his country (Congo) that there had been for many centuries. Even with the political leadership of democracies which in fact tended to represent (wanted to represent) social and ethical or even pacifist attitudes, military intervention is regularly started or strengthened (Red-Green government in Germany: Kosovo war 1998/99; George W. Bush: Iraq war and contempt for human rights). Not to mention the countless politicians and regimes for whom human rights are less important, or even the dictators and the military groups who hold power in different corners of the world and use this repressively, if they think it is necessary. The National Socialists tried to wipe out the Jewish population in Europe, Stalin and the Khmer Rouge became mass murderers in the name of communism.

Also noteworthy is the fact that the world is full of alliances between progressive democratic forces and powers which do not respect human rights or basic democratic rights (USA and Saudi Arabia, USA and the Egyptian military, strategic alliances in the Cold War). Relevant motives here are securing access to resources (e. g. oil), striving to maintain or expand political and economic influence, the arms trade.

If one compares the behaviour of animals in the general struggle for survival with that of humans, then we cannot fail to mention which new dimensions have been realised by general murder amongst human beings. The scientific-technical revolution has resulted in the development of weapons which can very effectively, or also very agonisingly, injure and kill a higher number of people. And these weapons are used. Human beings have succeeded in producing extraordinarily effective combat and military equipment. Usually this could still be a reasonably sensible option, if at the same time the appropriate responsibility is dealt with consistently. Unfortunately, however, it is shown again and again that this is not so. Time and again, the life and health of many people is damaged by the use of modern weapons.

No human being on earth can today be sure that he will not shortly be injured or killed by a gun, a chemical weapon, nuclear weapon, and possibly in the company of a larger number of fellow human beings.

There are many different reasons for these atrocities. However, a partial shortage of resources and population growth may be some of the most important factors for this development. Species' struggle for survival has changed so much with humans that the risk of an impending shortage of resources, which could also result from territorial constraints, leads to a general pursuit of power and influence. It is considered to be just and equitable for all available means to be used in order to enforce the claim to power. The development of increasingly powerful, effective resources and tools which can serve this purpose has become one of the most important motivations for human actions. In many countries, military expenditure has an important place in the budget. Scientific research is largely promoted to develop modern weapons, and for other military-strategic purposes.

Establishing a claim to power militarily is just the last resort – which, however, is unfortunately used much too often. The great game for power and influence also shaped or motivated behaviour in many other spheres of social life, such as for example in the economy and in politics. Even cultural and religious processes are regularly involved. Historical events such as the Crusades, the Inquisition, the Cultural Revolution in China, are only the most obvious examples. Wherever cultural, religious, informational processes appear to be suitable to give an advantage to one's own class, one's own country, one's own ethnic group, one's own family, one's own grouping, they are regularly corrupted by the pursuit of power and influence.

This perception of the social processes is at first alien to the normal, down-to-earth, human being. It does not seem to be at all natural or God-given. However, all the terrible events which there have been in history, and all the evil conflicts which today shape the world, are deliberately caused by human beings.

1.4 Criminality, corruption, mafia-like structures

The global political drama is only at the upper end of the scale of shamefulness. Society is regularly characterised by deplorable behavioural patterns, at every level.

In many of the world's countries, daily life is characterised by criminality and the influence of mafia-like alliances, or by militias or oligarchies. Here the practices range from the subtle infiltration of healthy social structures, to corruption and blackmail, up to more or less brutal force.

These actions appear to be regularly correlated with poverty. Everywhere where human beings live in poverty and dependency, criminal schemes seize space. But prosperous societies also see themselves permanently exposed to the danger of criminal and corrupt actions. One can assume that here as well, life is not characterised by pure integrity, but the level at which the game takes place here is characterised more by refinement, and the camouflage is more professional.

A basic rule seems to be that lifestyles that are characterised by selfishness, criminality and corruption thrive in secrecy. In contrast, everywhere where public attention is not far away, or where at least a few people sometimes peer in, the incentive for modes of behaviour which are characterised by cooperativeness and altruism tends to grow. Where one presents oneself, reveals one's own attitude under one's own name, there are incentives for integrity.

Conversely, the rule also applies that pure motives are at least aimed at being perceived as such in the community. Where this does not happen, this can lead to the atrophy of behaviours which are beneficial to the community – and thereby to an increase in negative events.

Where one can hide, criminality, deceit, disloyalty, corruption etc. thrive; money has no smell and if one spends it, how it was earned can no longer be identified – that is a significant incentive for dishonest behaviour.

Criminality and corruption, which are established in many parts of the world or which even, to a great extent, define life in some regions, clearly result from extreme contrasts between very rich and more or less corrupt or criminal power elites, on the one hand, and sectors of the population living in great poverty, on the other. The fact that the lust for money, wealth and power in society counts for more than a peaceful life, characterised by modest civilised behaviour, must be responsible for the marked distortions that there are in the world in this regard.

1.5 *Market economy, Keynesianism, prosperity and growth*

The capitalist market economy is the model and the basis for social life in today's Western society. In competition with other social systems (e. g. communism) it has established itself as the most successful model which, at least in the context of the history of the last few centuries, has been able to mobilise the driving forces that are slumbering in society in a highly effective way. The capitalist market economy can be regarded as being closely related to the scientific-technical revolution, prosperity and the free democratic basic order.

In other words: the capitalist-market-based form of society is today seen by its supporters as the definitive basis for progress, prosperity and humanism – and perhaps not completely without good reason.

Furthermore, this form of society exerts an enormous and increasingly growing influence on social life across the world. It seems as though market-based globalisation does not stop at any border in the long term. The export of this model is at least partly due to its attractiveness. One can therefore assume that the growing global influence of the Western model also occurs because, inter alia, people find the blessings of the market economy attractive.

One of capitalism's success factors consists in the mechanisms of the market economy. Through the law of supply and demand, there is the possibility that human activities, which can definitely be motivated by self-interest, can nevertheless result in a benefit for society. This leads to the phenomenon that striving to want to be helpful to fellow human beings, which cannot be denied to humans, can in some way be linked to striving to protect one's own interests. This phenomenon is also called the "invisible hand" in the literature, the first descriptions of this go back to Adam Smith (see e.g. Chapter 1 "The invisible hand" in Conway 2012, 5ff.).

There is no doubt that the law of supply and demand has characterised world history very strongly, at the latest from the 19th century. That in some countries today it is a fundamental basis for the fact that a life characterised by prosperity, democracy, self-determination and many years of peace is possible, can also scarcely be denied. At the same time, capitalism was always very controversial, and it was also clear that in some aspects it produced very bad fruit.

The development of the capitalist society has been influenced by a great variety of leading ideas. But in the last century some special theories became particularly important. Keynesianism is one of these. "It was the responsibility of government to kick-start the economy by borrowing cash and spending it, hiring public-sector staff and pouring cash into public infrastructure projects - for example, building roads and railways, hospitals and schools. [...] According to Keynes, the extra cash spent by government would filter through the economy. For example, building a new motorway creates work for construction firms, whose employees go out and spend their money on food, goods and services, which in turn helps keep the wider economy ticking over." (Conway 2012, 40) The intention is that increasing national debts, used to direct money into the economy, can be compensated later on – at least partially – by rising tax revenues.

In the past, however, despite or also partly because of Keynesianism, there was increasing inflation with consequences which could no longer be combated by renewed state expenditure and debt. Keynesianism is also still important in political decisions today where, however, it is subordinate to more modern economic schools of thought.

And it is Keynesianism that plays a certain role in a phenomenon that should here be called the neurasthenia of economic growth. Further important components are rapid acclimatisation to constantly increasing prosperity, as well as the short-sighted political actions in the most successful Western democracies, promoted by short legislative periods.

The word "neurasthenia" stands for weak nerves in humans. It is a concept that is out of date, not least because there is no really clear definition or diagnosis. But in relation to the nerve of public life in the affluent society, it can also be used quite well as satire, because of this lack of definition. Touching this nerve is nowadays a difficult thing to do, but it is also at the same time the most fundamental sport to which politics is subject.

Neurasthenia of economic growth means, in simple terms, that with prosperity, the more it grows, the more, also, there is a diktat that it must continue to grow. News that does not fit into this pattern is accepted even less by society, the higher the general prosperity – it seems then to involve much more the danger of a destabilisation of society.

Poor societies are constantly subject to the danger of destabilisation for objective reasons and bad news is normal. This is a "strength" which by implication rich societies do not have.

A range of consequences results from the neurasthenia of economic growth. First a positive consequence should be mentioned: growth results in constant incentives for efforts to further develop the social exchange process. In principle nothing can be said to contradict this, and therefore here is an important reason why some countries have to date achieved quite a high level of prosperity. However, it is also important to question the price to be paid for this – whether until now, or in the future, or in distant countries (this will be examined again later).

Together with prosperity, social models have emerged in which the social protection of underprivileged citizens is an important foundation. In principle this is a categorically positive development. However, in times of economic or demographic recession a problem of funding arises from this. Set-backs, which are occasionally unavoidable in this respect, are therefore reluctantly announced in plain language. Measures are much more likely to be taken which temporarily preserve the status quo. Even if the facade can never be sustained, nevertheless, with the desire to preserve social peace, there is a pressure which significantly hinders clear, open communication in society.

A decisive factor is the situation that politicians are only in office for short legislative periods, and afterwards they are no longer accountable for their positions and their decisions. Certainly they must also usually think about their future reputation. But in this respect society has a relatively short memory. Furthermore, with changing power structures it often happens that the consequences of one's own actions become a stumbling block for political opponents in the subsequent government. So there is considerable pressure to take measures which bring short-term success, but whose long-term effects can hardly be seen. One aspect in this is also that long-term effects are more difficult to measure and are less transparent. They are even less attributable to a political power, as changing occupants of government offices are involved in all long-term actions.

Short-sighted actions are therefore almost demanded. The fashionable word "sustainability" characterises efforts to escape this pressure, which are certainly also well-intentioned in part, but which instead appear to be powerless.

In addition to the offer of social protection, the sensitivity of the capitalist system to economic weaknesses also plays a crucial role. The entire structure really requires constant growth. The smallest sign of a recession, even the smallest doubt about the progress of the economy, can be intensified in a panicky way and lead to a profound crisis. Respect should always be paid to the pressures of the market. As long as this occurs, the market economy can be kept on the right track for a certain period of time.

Keynesianism would normally require that in times of economic boom, the economic margin is developed which is needed as a countermeasure in times of crisis. This is also true of the social systems – it should thus be possible to achieve a certain continuity that in good times one treats good deeds relatively cautiously, so that in bad times no excessive cuts are necessary. However, the pressure for short-sightedness has a consequence, that correspondingly clever economic activity is not opportune. In fact there is little opposition to the temptation to appease markets and social awareness at any time using the drug of good deeds.

So today an unprincipled and short-sighted handling of state debt is absolutely socially acceptable. Furthermore, deregulation of the markets, releasing the capitalist economic system from as many chains as possible, and measures to apparently strengthen or rescue the monetary system, are popular. Many of the measures which have been taken in the most recent past are thoroughly sensible or necessary. Many are controversial. However, overall there is the tendency for the economic and the financial system to increasingly be released from tangible principles and real values. State debt grows to dizzying heights – possible repayment is questionable and in part not even debatable any more. The virtual market values of companies in part lack any real basis. Central banks partially pump amounts of money into the system, which make inflation rates, which are still temporarily moderate, already appear today to be largely unreal and unbelievable. With the aid of high frequency trade, on the stock exchange virtual values, which are the culmination of the gigantic bubble of illusions, are conjured up out of nothing.

Earlier the capitalist system also operated without these gigantic exaggerations and it would not necessarily collapse if the pace was slightly more moderate and closer to reality. However, dealing with the capitalist system, characterised by the general neurasthenia, led to the administration of increasingly strong drugs and to a competition of an accelerating distance from reality. This is quite convenient and today it still seems to function reasonably well, but this clearly therefore calls into question the future more than is absolutely necessary.

1.6 Neoliberalism and contemporary capitalism

Another important economic school is known as monetarism. It is mainly based on the work of Milton Friedman of the University of Chicago. "The growth rate of an economy, argued Friedman, could be determined by controlling the amount of money being printed by central banks. Print more cash and people would spend more, and vice versa." (Conway 2012, 44)

As a consequence of this school, many central banks received the authority for autonomous control of the money supply, independent of politicians. This strategy worked out well, to a certain extent, and it made a significant contribution to the pronounced development in prosperity in Western countries after the Second World War. However, this Chicago school and its success are, on the one hand, now being questioned as a result of the increasingly careless application of the most important of its rules (see previous section). On the other hand, it simultaneously became the most important source of a phenomenon which is called neoliberalism, and which can be linked to the many evil excesses which are caused by contemporary capitalism.

Neoliberalism and the Chicago school stand for certain trends which are particularly characteristic of contemporary capitalism. However, they are not the only drivers of current developments, and there are quite different characteristics of the market-based system. Nevertheless, it seems to be sensible and necessary to highlight a few characteristic parameters of contemporary capitalism.

The success of the market-based system is essentially based on the invisible hand, the law of supply and demand, on confirmation of the right to property, man's individualistic image, and on close coaction with the free democratic order. However, an important factor should also, above all, be pluralism, which in the end enables competition and the scientific-technical revolution. Social life is based on interactions which take place on many different levels, such as, for example, culture, science, economy, public opinion, politics. On each of these levels, the question is consistently asked of whether a fruitful development is possible, and the answer essentially depends on to what extent diversity and pluralism are allowed and are a reality. Successful competition is then particularly possible if a variety of offers and alternatives is continually available. The successful further development of a system is then obstructed if this variety goes below a certain threshold.

Applied to the economic system this means, for example, that competition can only function if many competitors are active in the relevant market segments, which can to some extent match one another. Applied to the political system this means, for example, that there should, if at all possible, always be real alternatives for political decisions which one can choose between. In relation to the neoliberal trend, both are badly affected.

It has long been clear that the development of concentrations of power, as well as of monopolies or oligopolies, is not beneficial for social life. To combat the negative effects there are, inter alia, cartel offices, which occasionally prevent mergers or even break up large corporate groups. But first of all, in many countries, competition law is increasingly being weakened through small steps, and secondly the national agencies and governments are increasingly no match for large corporations which operate internationally.

It would be a good idea to take account of this imbalance and, subsequently, to strive to deploy the actions of the state on economic and cartel policy in an appropriate way. It is absolutely necessary to strengthen national politics and legislation in this respect, as well as to organise oneself internationally to such an extent that one can stand up to the large corporations. Only in this way can pluralism be saved, which again is the condition for the invisible hand and economic dynamism to be able to have an effect.

However, what happens is the opposite. It is precisely in connection with the neoliberal school of thought that power and influence is increasingly surrendered to multinational corporations. Colin Crouch (2011) states on this subject:

In Chapter 1 “The Previous Career of Neoliberalism”:

> “Under Chicago deregulation economics, US law would come no longer to see competition as a *process* that would maintain in existence large numbers of firms, near-perfect markets and widespread consumer choice. Instead, competition was to be seen by both law courts and economic theorists in terms of its *outcome* as the destruction of small and medium-sized enterprises, the dominance of giant corporations and the replacement of the demotic idea of consumer choice by a paternalistic concern for ‘consumer welfare’.” (16f.)

In Chapter 2 “The Market and Its Limitations”:

> “At the centre of the neoliberal project stands a portrayal of the qualities of the market, in particular a contrast between efficient, customer-sensitive firms and incompetent, arrogant public services.” (24)

In Chapter 3 “The Corporate Takeover of the Market”:

> “The Chicago school sees consumer welfare as maximized when the overall level of wealth is raised in an economy, on the grounds that consumers’ welfare cannot be increased by reducing the quantity of resources. They are explicitly uninterested in the distribution of this wealth, in who actually holds it. To take an extreme case, imagine a set of mergers that increases efficiency in an industry but which reduces

competition to the point where prices to consumers rise, or services to customers deteriorate as suggested above in the example of declining redundant capacity. Provided the quantity of wealth for shareholders by the efficiency gains is greater than that lost to customers' welfare, as the economy overall is richer. If pressed on whether it matters if the actual wealth is held by shareholders or spread among consumers, they would probably say that much of it is bound to 'trickle-down' to everyone else; but more importantly they would certainly argue that this is merely a distributive question and of no concern to economic theory. They might acknowledge that we may have reasons for caring about distribution, but would then say that this is a matter for political action, not for economics." (61f.)

In this context there is the question of how the configuration of power appears in the leading western market economies.

It is these countries which in particular boast about the democratic political system in which governments elected by the people determine the country's fate through political decisions. On behalf of the people these governments, inter alia, also have to make decisions on how the social system is to be further developed, which role the market should play, and how the balance between the development of competition and social concerns is to be justified. Here the intention is that the government is acting on behalf of the people as a whole, namely on behalf of all social classes, ethnicities and regions. This can result in certain distributions of power, with the risk of the oppression of minorities by majorities, although in advanced countries this is forbidden by the constitution as illegitimate behaviour. It remains to be seen how well that actually functions – that is not the issue here at the moment. However, what is certainly not wanted are power structures in which a minority has a disproportionate influence, or in which the majority no longer significantly determines policy, or in which it increasingly only appears to do this. However, it is precisely this trend that is being observed. Governments submit less and less to the people as sovereign, and more to the influence of large corporations, enforced by lobbying and blackmail.

It should not be claimed here that that was not always already a common phenomenon in capitalism. Yet, with the current trend towards neoliberalism and the imbalance mentioned between large corporations and governments, this trend and the respective effects of this are still intensifying significantly. What is particular about this is also that this trend is to a large extent publicly discussed and accepted. However, at the same time, this means that democratic values are betrayed more or less openly.

Crouch (2011) comes to the following conclusions on this:

Under the headline "Conclusion" in Chapter 4 "Private Firms and Public Business":

> "Political debate concentrates on 'state versus market'; if the firm is considered, it tends to be assimilated, by supporters and critics alike, to the market. But we have now seen how that is not the case; the market does not always require the firm, and vice versa.
>
> […]
>
> Neoliberalism departs astonishingly from both the political and economic legacy of liberalism in not seeing any problem in a close relationship between

> firms and the state, provided the influence runs from firms to the state and not vice versa. The first error of this position is not to realize that firms try to influence the state precisely because they then want that influence to turn back onto the economy, to grant them favours.
>
> When neoliberals do draw critical attention to uncomfortably close, competition-inhibiting relations between government and individual firms, it is because they have seen an ostensibly easy remedy: the complete disengagement of the state." (94f.)

In Chapter 7 "Values and Civil Society":

> "The previous chapters of this book have demonstrated that this familiar opposition of market and state is becoming threadbare, for two main reasons. First, where the neoliberal political right points to 'markets' it is often really indicating corporations. Second, the state, seen for so long by the left as the source of countervailing power against markets and corporations, is today likely to be the committed ally of giant corporations, whatever the ideological origins of the parties governing the state." (145)

It should not be claimed here that large corporations are in complete control. That would be an extremist assumption that could result in extremist reactions. But, according to Crouch (2011, x), it should be stated that the people's destiny is determined by at least the four-way configuration people – state – market – giant corporations, and that the giant corporations here play such an eminent role, which in fact may not be so good, and which is actually not intended on this scale. One can also state that small or nationally established companies can very well be attributed to the market and its beneficial effect on prosperity and democracy. In contrast, giant corporations have an effect which essentially increases so-called consumer welfare, although in a questionable way, and mainly for the benefit of those fellow human beings who are already extremely rich.

In any criticism of large corporations and the trend towards neoliberalism it should, however, not be forgotten that the increase in power and influence of the large corporations is ultimately only aided and made possible by the majority of citizens. The fact that a capitalist social order is predominant is predicated in liberal democratic countries on the will of the electorate. The trend towards neoliberalism is also continually sanctioned by democratic elections, and politics – not least on behalf of the people – has manoeuvred itself into the position in which it finds itself today. The loss of the only major opposition to the Western model, in the form of the Eastern Bloc, which occurred in the last century, may also have contributed to the increased acceptance of neoliberal trends.

Furthermore, one must consider that large corporations only become large through the purchasing decisions of consumers. Seen in this way, their success is well-deserved, and is based on broad consent. But it is often forgotten that certain transgressions should be countered in a timely way.

If one adheres to the conclusion that large corporations today have disproportionate and still growing influence, this is therefore particularly problematic because a priori no ethical behaviour can be expected from this element of power. The motivation for ethical behaviour always comes from the people, and it can be endowed with power and influence in two ways:

- Politics enforces ethical needs on behalf of the people.
- Through the power of consumers, corporations feel obliged to simulate ethical behaviour as part of marketing strategies. In extreme cases this can result in them actually behaving ethically, in part.

On the relationship between ethics and giant firms, Crouch (2011) concludes:

In Chapter 5 "Privatized Keynesianism":

> "It must be remembered that when we speak of owners of giant firms in the contemporary economy we no longer refer to the idea of entrepreneur owners or even of institutional shareholders who maintain long-term relations with senior managers. Under shareholder maximization, the role of owners is to look at share prices alone. Actual shareholders delegate their decision-making to traders acting for them who take interest only in the secondary market for a firm's shares – on the extreme velocity of which their own rewards depend. The powerful players in the financial markets do not 'hold' shares at all; they just trade them. The connection between ownership of a business and concern for even the financial aspects of its actual performance has become highly attenuated. And yet this shareholder interest remains the only legitimate interest in a corporation in the eyes of Anglo-American corporate law." (106)

It remains to be seen whether, in addition to the ethical question, in particular the question of respect for consumers, employees and citizens, it is also about any other form of consideration. Just as corporations are a priori not considerate towards this, after all, already privileged group of people, neither do they show a priori any form of consideration towards the environment or towards human beings and people who do not play an important role in their economic network. Large corporations must first be forced to be considerate at all.

Colin Crouch draws the conclusion that civil society can still be considered as an important factor to promote the common good. In relation to the four poles of the configuration of power mentioned above, – people, state, market, giant corporations – we can see civil society as affiliated to the people. In Chapter 7 "Values and Civil Society" Crouch (2011, 152ff.) writes under the headline "Civil Society": "This brings us to an important concept: civil society, which, in its early twenty-first-century sense, deals with this question of both diversity and balance. […] We can consider at least five kinds of groups which are the quintessential actors in civil society, in large part driven by values." In the following he specifies these five groups:

- The political parties.
- The religions.
- The campaigning groups.
- The voluntary and charitable sector.
- Occupational groups, where they have developed sets of autonomously derived values.

Civil society can exert influence through a variety of organisations (e. g. NGOs), associations, protest, citizen and opposition movements, but also Internet blogs. Stéphane Hessel applauds the Occupy Movement and calls for civil disobedience and engagement in civil society (cf. Hessel 2011). People employed by large corporations also have scope for decision-making, which they can use in some way or another, even if the highest priority here is always shareholder value, marketing concepts and public relations. In this regard, Colin Crouch refers to the concept of "Corporate Social Responsibility", which "was developed by firms themselves as something that they did to fulfil certain obligations to society" (Crouch 2011, 134). It is therefore possible to oppose the a priori unethical behaviour of international large corporations with a certain political authority. For their part, the large corporations have a lot of money available for this which can, however, ultimately not be used to buy everything. On the other hand, the civil society groupings have the advantage that they can often claim ethical maxims for themselves where it is, however, not always certain that these are justified.

All initiatives and movements in civil society are accorded great importance, but what is critical here is the behaviour of each individual citizen. In the end, however, the goal must also always be to once again establish better trust in politics, because the only known solution for reasonably untainted control of a people's destiny consists in democratically legitimated political activity.

Finally Crouch (2011) makes the following conclusions in Chapter 8: "What's Left of What's Right?":

> "These arguments about civil society are not new. Back in the 1950s the late US economist J. K. Galbraith (1952) wrote of the need for groups of 'employees, consumers, savers and shareholders' to exert a balancing power against corporate might. In the late 1990s Giuliano Amato (1997) ended his study of antitrust law by explicitly recalling Galbraith's words and commending them to our own day. Slightly later the British political scientist David Marquand (2004) wrote of the 'need to redress the balance between the commercial invasion of government and a top-down

state by reasserting civic muscle', through the moral commitments of an engaged citizenry. It is a remarkable fact that all three of these men have been political insiders, at different periods and in different countries. Galbraith was a central member of the group around the US presidency of J. F. Kennedy in the early 1960s; Amato has in recent years held the posts of prime minister and other senior offices in the Italian state; Marquand was a British member of parliament in the 1970s and subsequently played an important role in the European Commission. Yet none of them suggests that we try to resolve the issues at stake through the formal political process. They direct us to that wider world of civil society.

This is both bad and good news. It is bad, because it amounts to pitting against the might of both corporate and government institutions the 'power of the powerless'. Also, in the end much civil action has to find a response at the level of government if it is to get anywhere. This is the sobering message of a book by Debra Spini (2006) on post-national civil society (*La societá civile postnazionale*). Having opened up to us an exciting vista of citizens' actions extending across national boundaries, she reminds us of the continued presence of the indispensible gatekeeper, the solidly national democratic state. And the political party, manipulated though that institution has become, remains a major gatekeeper en route to that primary gatekeeper.

But the news is good, because it shows us that there are things that ordinary citizens can do. I said in the Preface that this book is directed at those who have to cope with the world rather than those who try radically to reshape it. But coping can include campaigning

> successfully for many minor victories. Governments do often intervene to protect citizens from corporate abuse, as official campaigns against smoking and unhealthy foods, which have, if anything, been strengthened in recent years, demonstrate. Such cases give us hope. These government actions can usually be traced back to small groups of poorly funded but passionately committed professionals and people of good will. Firms that boast of their green or fair trade credentials did not dream up these ideas in their marketing departments; they were responding to serious customer pressure, which was in turn responding to campaigning by small numbers of concerned activists in ecological groups and trade unions. There is no need for defeatism. Rarely before in human history has there been so little deference shown to authority, so much demand for openness, so many cause organizations, journalists and academics devoting themselves to criticizing those who hold power and holding up their actions to scrutiny. New electronic forms of communication are enabling more and more causes to express themselves in highly public ways." (176ff.)

As stated, in his conclusions Colin Crouch addresses those fellow human beings "who have to cope with the world rather than those who try radically to reshape it". This conciliatory handling of the still quite deplorable imbalances and conditions in contemporary market economies is not unwise and Colin Crouch's moderate attitude is admirable. However, the author of this book cannot share this restraint. With things as they are, it is not enough not to want to radically change the world!

If one were to look at the reality, which this and other sections of the Chapter "Culture or disaster?" attempt to specify in a rudimentary way, then there is, however, the imperative to fundamentally change something in this world. A major problem of our era is the belief, which largely prevails in the West, that the capitalist market economy and the consumer society is the highest form of society that one can aspire to, that they offer the only solution available today to build a fair society, that only certain adjustments and reforms are needed to achieve a better outcome. Of course, it is not completely wrong to want to act in this way.

But this is not enough.

First of all it is inefficient if many small groups and lone warriors, isolated from each other, consistently wear themselves out with individual activities in order to pit themselves against the giants of the economy and their allies in governments. It would be better if one could also oppose the system of the global market, and of big business which systematically profits from it, using leverage in the form of a system, a paradigm, a common strategy.

Secondly, the imbalance between civil society and corporations is only one partial aspect in the drastic misguided development which human society is following at the moment. Taking a dispassionate view, a global culture change is required in order to avert a greater home-made human disaster. The absurdity of unbridled capitalism is the crucial reason for a large part of the extreme global differences between poverty and wealth, of global environmental destruction and of the many wars and terror attacks. The dominance of large corporations, whose highest principle does not envisage a human or considerate management style, characterises human activity across the globe in a way which, in questions of humanity, environmental protection, and resource conservation, is indicated by extensive ignorance.

Not only supporters of capitalism and neoliberalism are profoundly fixated on the issue of the monetary economy. All other powers in politics and civil society are also in the corresponding maelstrom. In every engagement in social, cultural and environmental aspects, the discourse is always ostensibly polarised towards the question of the provision and application of the relevant financial resources – that is very quickly the focal point of the discussion. It is known that there are also still intangible aspects, but this often becomes an irrelevance.

The market-based society makes itself highly dependent on the consumption of goods which, together with the simultaneously accelerating growth in product variety and the number of consumers, results in an extreme exploitation of global resources, which is constantly speeding up. Here, consumer prosperity only acts as the most important projection screen for the pursuit of happiness. That there are other possibilities is demonstrated, for example, by Buddhists, as well as by many other fellow human beings, who, in terms of the ownership of goods, traditionally apply slightly more modest standards. From this point of view, the consumer society is a question of belief. And, in relation to current trends, one can only state that that is an extremely disastrous belief.

Even in its very own domain, the economy, capitalism itself is consistently severely tested. The speculative dealing of the monetary and financial system is brought to a head with increasing audaciousness for so long until it can no longer adequately fulfil the important function that it has for social life, or even completely collapses. A variation in the decline is also the pledging of multi-billion euro sums which are not available in the kitty, but only a bill of exchange for expected tax revenue in the future. Of course, then the subscribed losers in particular, but also many kinds of winner, have to suffer the consequences. The obsession with growth and greed is partly so strongly developed that a collapse in society, with all its dire consequences such as radicalisation and war, is accepted, quite apart from the collapse of the environment and conditions in the poor countries of the world.

1.7 *Globalisation, poverty and hunger*

The words "capitalism" and "market economy" are terms for a form of society that has developed in particular in Europe and in the so-called Western world as the successor to feudalism and mercantilism. There are a variety of cultures around the world for which, for historical reasons, the transition to the market economy is much less logical and obvious. Of course, however, in these cultures as well life is constantly characterised by the debate about material needs and relevant deficiencies.

Ownership of products and goods and individualism may not have the importance everywhere that it has in Western culture, but besides, there are also basic needs, the fulfilment of which is also set at a new level by the market economy. Ideally, market-based affluent societies produce an environment in which the fulfilment of basic needs is no longer a problem for all people. Many Western countries are, at least temporarily, clearly approaching this ideal state of affairs. In other cultures this is often much less self-evident. Furthermore, modern product diversity and luxury is also rather attractive, which people in most cultures cannot necessarily resist in the long run.

This means that the market economy is an export success and in principle it is welcomed by many people.

At the same time, a constant stimulus for growth arises from the principles and laws of the market-based system, and with it a demand for expansion, as well as an absolute compulsion to increase the exploitation of globally available resources.

Particularly also in relation to the considerable successes of scientific-technological progress, it is therefore logical that world events are increasingly characterised by the capitalist-market-based system, and that this development, which can be summarised as globalisation, has gained momentum.

Unfortunately, however, it is the case that many cultures are traditionally much less compatible with the market economy than, for example, those in which Protestant and Calvinist ethics, as well as the Enlightenment, have played a role. A completely different, but even more serious problem, is the fact that the element of ruthlessness is inherent in the capitalist compulsion for expansion. It is true that expansion projects are carried out by people who are employed in the relevant companies, administrations and associations, or who act on their behalf. However, the logic of expansion follows the principle of profit maximisation – often with a short-term horizon, which all those involved have to follow. Ethical behaviour may be of major importance for many of the players, but when facing a crucial decision, shareholder value or the expected profits often displace all other considerations.

The results are extreme distortions in the world of progressive globalisation.

It would have been perfect if the principle of the synergy between self-interest and service to fellow human beings that has in fact also led to the success of capitalism in the form of the "invisible hand" had been more effective when disseminated around the world. However, the reality appears to be that globalisation does not make itself dependent on such an approach. In addition to the good examples of prosperous economies which developed in formerly poor countries, there are also many negative examples.[1] Globalisation in part acts more like a modern continuation of colonialism than the stronghold of a progressive and humanist affluent society.

This closes the circle on the theme of the "striving for power, violence and wars". After an endless story of political conflicts, the thirst for power, of violent arguments, of colonialism etc., there now follows a story about the dominance of big business, for which all means are justified to assert its hegemonial ambitions and its demands.

A few examples and evidence from the more recent past are brought together below:

India:

> Many global corporations now have their subsidiaries in India and many Indian companies can be classed as global big business. Indian software developers and technology companies are in great demand and other industries are also developing strongly. At the same time, a large proportion of the population live in extreme poverty. "Almost half the most seriously (and permanently) malnourished people on the earth live in slums in Mumbai (Bombay), Calcutta, New Delhi, in the tribal areas or the isolated rural areas of Orissa,

[1] In the heartlands of capitalism as well, the invisible hand does not automatically have a positive effect. There are in fact constant arguments here to assess and regulate the effects, which typically also include exploitation and poverty.

Uttar Pradesh and Bengal. Out of a total of one billion people worldwide who are suffering from a serious permanent shortage of adequate nutrition, 382 million of them are in India." (Ziegler 2011, 97)

Nigeria (based on 2009, see also Mättig 2012):

Nigeria is rich in resources such as natural gas, coal, but particularly oil. Nigeria is the "eighth largest global crude oil producer and the largest in Africa" (Ziegler 2011, 128), and the most important regional power. All large oil companies have a presence here and operate oil platforms. At the same time, extreme poverty and a shortage of resources prevail in the country. Even petrol is scarce. A military power elite rules the country. Life as a whole is characterised by corruption, extortion and violent assaults. Road blocks, with which the police supplement their income, drive up the gap between farmers' income and the cost of food in the towns (cf. Ziegler 2011, 128ff.). The oil companies deal with the risk of oil leaks and environmental damage here with considerably less care than, for example, in similar cases in the USA. Fishing grounds and drinking water resources in the Niger Delta are, for example, unscrupulously destroyed. The power elites know how to take their vast wealth abroad safely, while they do not manage to reach the lowest minimum standards in education, infant mortality, life expectancy, the supply of drinking water, public sanitation and income. Thus, Nigeria has become a "factory of hate" (Ziegler 2011, 125) against the West.

Countries of the South:

"Since 1975 fifty-eight countries of the South have become impoverished. They contain the *Bottom Bil-*

lion, the one billion people who form the bottom layer of poverty. Most of these countries belong to the ACP countries." The ACP countries include a large number of developing countries in Africa, the Caribbean and the Pacific region. This also includes Nigeria. These countries are encouraged by the European Union concluding agreements with them, "which grant the poorest countries certain privileges". This is to overcome the effects of the colonial era. However, conditions are in part imposed on them which result in them "not being able to develop any national industrialisation policy whatsoever". But the West wants to "enforce investment agreements so that the countries of the South will open up for the transcontinental private companies of the West". (citations: Ziegler 2011, 88–91).

USA foreign policy:

"The USA's foreign policy is, under Obama as well, largely dominated by geostrategic interests, in other words by the Pentagon, the CIA and their practices. The main reason: despite its comparatively low population of 300 million, the USA is by far the biggest industrial power in the world. Twenty-five per cent of all industrial goods produced in a year are produced by Americans. The dominant raw material is crude oil: every day the USA consumes 20 million barrels. Of these only eight million are produced domestically; twelve million, so over sixty per cent, have to be supplied from abroad, in most cases from unstable, strife-torn regions (the Middle East, the Persian Gulf, Nigeria, amongst others). According to Amnesty International (Report 2009) many strategic allies of the USA (Uzbekistan, Saudi Arabia, Israel, Kuwait, Nigeria, Columbia) are among countries that are guilty of ongoing serious human rights abuses" (Ziegler 2011, 110).

Haiti:

"Haiti is today the poorest country in Latin America and the third-poorest country in the world. In Haiti, rice is the staple food. In the early 1980s, Haiti was self-sufficient in rice. Working terraced fields and the wet lowlands, Haitian farmers were protected from foreign dumping by an invisible wall: a tariff of 30 percent on imported rice. But over the course of the 1980s, Haiti was subjected to two programs of structural adjustment. Under orders from the IMF, the protective tariff was reduced from 30 to 3 percent. American rice, which is heavily subsidized by the U.S. government, flooded into Haitian towns and villages, destroying the country's rice production and, as a consequence, the way of life of tens of thousands of rice farmers. Between 1985 and 2004, Haitian imports of foreign rice, mainly American and heavily government-subsidized, increased from 15,000 tons to 350,000 tons annually. At the same time, local rice production collapsed, declining from 124,000 tons to 73,000 tons.

Since 2000, the Haitian government has had to spend more than 80 percent of its meager revenues to pay for imported food. And the destruction of rice farming has caused a massive exodus from the countryside. The overcrowding of Port-au-Prince and the country's other big cities has led to the disintegration of public services. In short, Haitian society has been totally turned upside down, weakened, made more vulnerable than ever before by the effects of the IMF's neoliberal policies. And Haiti has been reduced to a beggar state, subject to foreign laws. Coups

> d'etat and social crises have followed inevitably, one after another, throughout the last twenty years.
>
> Normally, the 9 million people of Haiti consume 320,000 tons of rice per year. When world prices for rice tripled in 2008, the Haitian government was unable to import enough food. In Cite Soleil, between the hill that dominates Port-au-Prince and the Caribbean – one of the largest shantytowns in Latin America – hunger began to prowl the streets." (Ziegler 2013, 124f.)

With globalisation, a process has started which, from a humanist view, can only be described as an absolute aberration. Particularly blatant is the fact that, in this process, democratic affluent countries, which are supposed to stand for such fine things as human rights, personal rights, humanism, the Enlightenment, peace etc., systematically act in such a way that these values are betrayed all the more consistently the further a region or a culture is apparently distant from its own interests.

The field is left open here to two mechanisms, in the sense that human, humanistic motivations are subordinated to them:

- The law of supply and demand, the invisible hand and the market economy principle, respectively. The belief in market mechanisms, which is partly justifiable as it is an important basis for development, which has led in part to prosperity and democracy, is so great that negative effects are willingly accepted as a necessary evil.
- The principle of shareholder value. The application of this principle, in particular in relation to international big business, is attributed to the power of continuously developing prosperity, and it is seen as

sensible or even as mandatory to maximise prosperity on the basis of this principle.

The belief in these mechanisms is so deeply rooted in the Western world that they are regularly given priority over normal human considerations. In the enormous global system which determines peoples' lives particularly strongly, even preferentially, in the form of large corporations, state apparatus and governments, people are indeed active but they systematically organise their decisions in order to pay homage to the principles mentioned above. Of course, each of the people taking action in this system primarily follows human standards of evaluation. At the same time, however, it is also possible for constraints to occur regularly which make it necessary to abandon these standards of evaluation in favour of profits and expansive competition. It is accepted that this is the supreme reason, which ultimately wins in an emergency.

The capitalist system seeks growing markets. This could lead one to hope for a tendency that worldwide more and more people are involved in the market, and that they will be increasingly welcomed as participating members. Such a development is perhaps possible, but reality shows that it does not have to result from the capitalist principle. It is much more the case that capitalism is indifferent on how market growth is achieved. If a limited number of participants buy an increasing number of luxury goods it is, then, apparently comparable to growth from an increasing number of participants.

However, what is quite obviously urgently necessary is the fight for global resources. In this regard, the capitalist system knows no limits. It does not ask whether, in areas with an abundance of resources, beneficial political conditions for a market-based-democratic political system can be created. Large investments and the exploitation of resources have priority. With what human criteria this happens is of secondary importance.

In many regions of the world, however, the social system is traditionally characterised by family and clans, caste systems, particular social classes, ethnic groups. Countries which were exploited in colonial times also often have the problem that there are no longer any traditional roots on which a certain social solidarity could be based, or that artificial borders were drawn which conflict with ethnic conditions. Many poor regions thus have great difficulties in following a route which leads to adequate livelihoods for most citizens.

Quite a specific dimension of disaster regularly befalls regions which have the misfortune, in the context of a political-humanist vacuum, to have resources or capabilities which come to the attention of international investors. Here alliances are formed which provide inhuman powers with considerable resources to retain power and oppress the population. In general, there is the alternative here between a regime that rules with an iron fist, or a situation which is characterised by a disastrous mixture of corruption and crime. Because of the substantial financial resources that are thrown into the equation, the usual social differences grow into inhumane living conditions.

The investor community and the Western world end up as a rich wolf in sheep's clothing. They come in with the attitude of organisation, economic development, human rights, democracy, prosperity, wealth, the win-win situation, aid agencies, the UN, the IMF etc. But at the same time, they bring options in the rucksack with them, such as support for repressive, military, corrupt, criminal regimes and organisations, environmental pollution, destruction of the bases of autonomy, war. It is not the case that negative developments are pursued, but they are regarded as possibly necessary, and if in doubt, are accepted for the reason of profit maximisation.

People in the Western world would like to live in prosperity and peace, but at the same time they pay homage to a principle that knows no humanity. Furthermore, through scientific-technological progress the effects of this weakness are so enormous that world peace is constantly hanging in the balance, and recently the global collapse of the environment is also at risk. Of course, this is not intended, and most people operating within this system make an honest effort to behave in a humane way, and there is some evidence of successes in the direction of humanism and environmental protection. However, the problem is that the belief in the redemptive power of the principles of capitalism mentioned above is at least so strong that, in the name of these principles, it is allowed to continue along the path, afflicted by all these negative side effects, without any serious correction.

1.8 Bureaucracy, regulation mania and creativity

In conclusion, a few rather minor problems of affluence are mentioned here in passing.

The modern market-based society poses many new difficulties which barely played a prominent role before. Many people are involved in production processes and are forced to function more than to act. For many, the demands are increasingly complex and unmanageable. Another problem is lack of exercise, which is often enforced by modern work processes. This has various effects and consequences particularly, also, in the way in which people become ill. Part of the problem manifests itself in particular in an increased number of diseases, even epidemics, such as diabetes, depression, burnout, attention deficit disorder (ADD), cardiovascular disease, a tendency towards addictions etc.

Moreover, one can mention a problem that can in part be seen as related, the bureaucratisation of social processes. The rapid development of knowledge and the progressive control of increasingly complex technological processes have led to the constant complication of laws, general terms and conditions (GTC), rules and provisions. There is one particular aspect in relation to money and desired or existing wealth – the struggle to participate in the blessings of the financial world is deemed to be so important that increasingly, financial products and legal constructs that are not transparent and that are complex to manage are generally regarded as acceptable.

Overall this leads to a powerful constraint and a daily routine that resembles a treadmill. The reality of life is played out between the following two poles:

- The Coolness Pole

  This amounts to not taking a large part of the requirements seriously and either coolly ignoring these, signing these without reading them (e. g. GTC) or implementing these in a minimal way with no emotional involvement (e. g. certification dogmas).

- The Psycho Pole

  This amounts to at least one symptom of excessive demand. Examples are overeating and diabetes, depression, burnout, ADD, psychosomatic symptoms and somatisation disorders.

For the younger generation there is also a major contradiction between their natural fantasy world and the reality of everyday school life, as well as the requirement to integrate themselves, in the context of socialisation, in the straitjacket-like processes of everyday life.

In this way social processes act like a cage which contains people with creative potential in an unemotional mechanism of everyday life which forces them to work and which leaves many people ill and unhappy.

Another problem is the increasingly observed prevalence of dementia in affluent societies. It is clear that this trend results in particular from the demographic change which is taking place in these societies. However, the question of to what extent mental impairment plays a role in this, and whether one has to helplessly confront this phenomenon, should be clarified.

1.9 Short-sightedness of democracy

The short legislative periods of democracy inevitably and obviously result in policies that are much too short-sighted.

Normally, taking political decisions means balancing different interests and risks. As social life happens in reality, and not in a utopian affluent society or in a society in which there are enough so-called win-win situations, which can always be identified at an early stage, it is inevitable that political decisions can never satisfy all interests. In general, only a small part of the legislative period is available to implement this serious responsibility. In the last few months before an election, the scope for action once again vanishes in the populist constraints of the election campaign.

If there are debates and decisions on the consequences of analytical forecasts, or on systematically applied programmes and projects, the foundations for these can partly be traced back to preliminary work by the ministries. In the other, perhaps more significant part, however, they are based on contributions made by experts, who are more or less strongly involved in representing lobby interests. In fact, this means that a variety of competences from the human portfolio are incorporated in political decisions, but this only operates at the cost of the directive influence of particularly powerful interest groups. In addition, it should be noted that every client is at the same time also a member of the electorate, and that, through disregard for certain imperatives, sentiments can be activated at any time that are disastrous for a politician or his party. In principle, politicians are facing the responsibility of using expertise and paying attention to sentiments, without following the manipulative components[2] that are contained in this too much. This amounts to balancing on a knife-edge or squaring the circle.

From this one can assume that politics, even in the best democracy, is regularly plagued by a certain shortsightedness. On the one hand this appears in relation to future prospects and, on the other hand, to the balance of interests to be represented. With both perspectives politics regularly easily fails the possible optimum.

However, in relation to the question of how these deficiencies can be remedied, good advice is expensive. Nevertheless one can, in any case, count oneself lucky if

[2] In just a few cases, hidden manipulation is certainly the result of really dishonest intentions, but it is, in fact, the legitimate function of lobbyists to point out the views of the interest groups to be represented, and thus to act professionally.

one can live in a country in which a distinctive democratic form of the constitution and political processes has already been fought for in the past.

In this sense, the short-sightedness of democracy is itself not a complete disaster. However, it is a reason why it is so difficult, even almost apparently impossible, to find suitable solutions to the pronounced deficiencies of human society, which get worse every year.

In addition to this very sympathetic description of the problem of short-sightedness, there are, as is known, substantial risks which could lead to an exacerbation of this problem. Thus in many cases the honest efforts of some of the citizens involved in the democratic process are confronted by actions such as corruption, deceit, extortion, crime, physical threats or overt violence. Democracies, which to a large extent have to fight such actions, consequently have considerably more blind spots regarding the systematic and fair organisation of society.

1.10 Is there a way out?

Ultimately there is a way out of the disaster. Human beings have shown a great ability to consistently find innovative ways to deal with difficulties and crises. Human culture will thus evolve in some form or other and there will also be solutions for every problem. However, it is also extremely important to continue to reflect on and analyse the changing social configuration, as well as to develop ideas and strategies which can provide suitable answers to each of the social problems that are posed.

The following chapters will try to make a contribution to the associated social discourse. These will first consider a few particular aspects of human nature, before conclusions are drawn from this for society and for possible approaches to solving the range of problems posed here.

2 The neural system

2.1 The human being as machine

First it should be emphasised that we are not talking here in any way about seriously seeing human beings as machines, or to put them on a level with these. The reverse is the case. However, the comparison with the machine should be made from the outset, so that later we can establish more precisely where the decisive difference is between a human being and a machine.

With a machine, or an automated production facility, we can distinguish four categories of elements in an abstract way:

1. Sensors, measuring systems etc., in other words features which provide information.
2. Actuators, control elements, process mechanisms, so elements which change/process/move something.
3. Electronic control units and data processing components, in other words elements which process information and control the interaction of elements.
4. The constructive structures and supply facilities, in other words everything needed to provide the other three categories of elements with the suitable environment and supply infrastructure. Simultaneously, the elements in categories 1, 2 and 3 can also provide a basis for the construction and preservation of structure and infrastructure.

The system of the human body offers certain analogies to this:

1. There are five senses – touch, hearing, sight, taste, smell –, through which information on the environment is processed via the peripheral receptors, affer-

ent nerve tracts and the relevant projection fields in the cerebrum.[3] Physiological processes within the body which activate signals in the nervous system must also be mentioned here.

2. Signal processing leads from the motor cerebral cortex via efferent nerve tracts to the muscles that are readily available, and is therefore responsible for any kind of activity. A further important category of elements are glands or vegetative control elements whose function can be influenced by neural processes.
3. The decisive part of signal processing is executed by the human brain. Here the cerebral cortex plays a prominent role in particular human abilities, but also systems that are located deeper are acknowledged to have an important contribution. There is also always signal processing at lower levels – e. g. in the form of reflex arcs in the spinal cord.
4. Finally there is the human body itself, with all its organs, blood and lymph vessels and bone skeleton.

Despite these analogies, there is something absurd about comparing man to a machine. In fact it is clear that humans or in fact all plants and animals as well are unique, that, to a certain extent, they have a fascination that the machine or the automated production facility completely lacks. It is thoroughly unacceptable to want to make a comparison.

However, the question about what the decisive difference actually is should be asked and discussed here.

[3] In fact there are other senses and more differentiated classifications. However, for the discussion of certain principles it is sufficient to initially refer to the five senses.

Is it the varied biological sophistication of animal and plant organisms? Yes, but if anything that is a gradual difference, which may be reduced by progress in scientific-technical developments.

Is it in the signal processing, in the processes which occur in the nervous system? Yes, of course! But what is it exactly?

If there is a decisive difference, then it is in the feelings and emotions with which living beings are provided, and with which machines are generally not provided. But how do emotions come about, how do they interact with control operations, and how can one describe the particular qualities of the biological and, in particular, human life that exist here?

2.2 The brain processor

Before being able to describe emotions, we must first go into more detail about the neural system. How does the human neural processor work? On what principles are its structures and activities based?

In general, neural processes function on the basis of impulses, which are partly electrically, partly chemically transmitted via neurons and synapses, and which are measurable as potential. Here, net-like connections between neurons, synapses, play an important role; in addition there are inhibitory, enhancing and feedback mechanisms. Signal processing generally occurs via complex modular systems, interconnected at multiple levels. In all processes, whether processes of perception, control or awareness, many areas of the brain are normally involved. Individually, these processes are extremely complex and researching these is a major field in which only small advances are consistently achieved using complex procedures.

In this sense, it is very difficult to make definite conclusions on how the brain processor functions. However, it is completely legitimate to describe a few important principles on the basis of current knowledge in an abstract way.

The processes largely follow the principles of control systems already described above, with sensors, actuators and control components. In simple terms, existing input signals, released by receptors and transported over afferent nerve pathways, feed control processes, which again lead to responses via efferent nerve pathways and muscles. Here the input signals released via the somaesthetic and vegetative (body awareness) interfaces, as well as the possibilities for influencing bodily functions provided via glands or vegetative control elements, also play an important role. A more interesting factor here is that, for receptors of all senses and areas of the body, there are positive projection fields in the cerebral cortex, and also that the afferent nerve pathways of all muscle groups can be assigned to particular areas of the so-called motor cortex (cf. also Chapters E1–E3 in Popper/Eccles 2006, 227ff.).

A major component of the control technology of machines or entire factories follows the principle that signals provoke reactions, and that here logical or control elements play a role which generate complex answers from the complex combinations of signal patterns and measurements. This principle finds an analogy in the human organism in the form of receptors, afferent nerve pathways, and sensory cortex fields on the one hand, muscles, efferent nerve pathways and motor cortex areas on the other, as well as signal processing in the cerebral cortex.

Here it is characteristic, both for machines and for animals and humans, that the connection logic which controls signal processing, and thus the answers, can be programmed. With a machine, software components are installed to this end, which consist of procedures explicitly programmed for this purpose. With animals and humans, an analogy is something like conditional reflexes or conditioned behaviour. However, this initially provides only a possible explanation for a comparatively primitive part of human nature, and also machine control technology generally exhibits qualities which go beyond this principle.

With systems engineering, the following should be considered in particular: First, there are self-activated processes. In this context should be mentioned, for example, concepts such as timer-control, agents, services etc. Here it is characteristic that procedures and information processing activities are realised which require no external impulse or signal. Second, data bases and data processing procedures should be referred to. These allow part of the information accumulating in the production or system control to be stored permanently, and to be used again selectively in later processes in a specific way. In this way, we obtain control technology which is active in a self activated way, and its reactions are not only knee jerk reactions, but it can also make competent decisions which are based on information from quite different points in time and activity phases. In principle, machines can therefore also “act”, and they can use a memory.

With animals and humans, it is largely clear that they always act in a self-activating way, and that they have both a short-term and a long-term memory. Here, the natural solutions for signal processing and storage look quite different from the comparable technical solutions in computer and control technology. Signals are transmitted as electro-chemical impulses via nerve pathways. Stimulus transmission occurs in connections between different nerve cells, the synapses, via transmitters, the neurotransmitters. The synapses in the cerebral cortex are largely changeable, and so provide the basis for flexible action programmes like conditional reflexes, as well as long-term memory. In contrast to computer technology, signal processing tends to occur here in analogue form, every signal can occur and be transmitted at different intensities.

This statement was deliberately relativised with the word “tends to”, since computer technology is no more solely digital than the nerve system is solely analogue. With computer technology, although all processes are based on binary coding, scalar dimensions also play a significant role, such as for example measured data or the values of volume and of brightness etc. With nervous systems, i.e. in the nerve cells, signal processing again takes place in the form of impulses or electrical waves (also called action potential). Depending on type, the transmission or blocking of impulses in the neighbouring neurons occurs in the synapses.

However, the concern here should not be the detail of the technical and natural principles on which the respective signal processing and storage is based. Instead, efforts should be made to draw a few significant analogies between animal and computer, between man and systems engineering, in order to then arrive at the fundamental differences.

2.3 *The Attention Assessor (AA) as central control unit*

There is also a certain similarity between technology and nature at the heart of the system, the central mechanism which controls information processing. In the computer this is the central processing unit. An instruction pointer executes actions which are filed as program code in the memory. The possible actions provide access to the main memory, the hard disk, hardware and interfaces, and the result is the processing of binary coded information, including the ability to send and receive code streams. Modern computer architectures are also able to process several programs simultaneously or in parallel (multi-threading, multiprocessor architecture, parallel computers).

In the brain processor there is – admittedly at quite an abstract level – a central control unit that is comparable to the computer processor, which is, however, less deterministically explored than the computer processor is deterministically synthesised. This means that we can disagree about the interpretation of the relevant research results. There is no reliable evidence on this issue, and we are dependent on forming hypotheses.

References to this central processing mechanism, to its mode of operation and its localisation are to be found, for example, in Popper/Eccles 2006 in section 62: "Hypothesis of Neuronal Happenings in Memory Storage" (394ff.). There is a description of a sub-system of the cerebrum, the essential elements of which are assumed to be mainly in the so-called limbic system, in the hippocampus and in other centrally located fields, as well as in the prefrontal cortex. In this system – at least when awake – signalling mechanisms are running continuously, largely controlling and evaluating the states of excitation in the brain via extensive connections to all other areas of the cerebral cortex. The patterns of signals that have been received once, and actions executed once, can be repeated cyclically. Here the central system only has the role of a conductor controlling stimuli, while the actual signal patterns are running where they originally occurred – in the cortex fields which serve perception, sensorimotor function, speech or other functions.

This system is of central importance for several features of performance, which are in particular attributed to the human brain. These relate to short- and long-term memory, to thinking and consciousness, and not least to control of attention and actions.

The term "Attention Assessor" (AA) will be introduced here for this system. Attention, because it controls the attention of neural processes to each one of several competing excitation patterns. Assessor, because the signal processes which take place in this system are also always inseparably linked to a continually occurring assessment, or because assessment is an essential part of any control process which derives from this system. Two things are always assessed:

- the neural procedures currently operating,
- attention to these procedures.

One particular feature of the AA is that it is able to simultaneously switch between different signal or excitation patterns. If a particular excitation pattern has for a time oscillated (resonated), the AA can again return to excitation patterns which were active before. Earlier patterns are preserved for a time in the form of weak, subliminal oscillations, and can be reactivated again later. In this way, the brain is enabled to simultaneously switch between different information processing procedures. This feature can be equated with the performance feature "Short-term memory". The storage time of this memory is generally given with times of less than one minute. However, this kind of memory also depends on the quantity and complexity of the information to be processed, so that in this regard it can also be called storage capacity. The analogy to the computer is the main memory.

When assessing the apparent narrowness of this kind of memory, it must be considered that the processes which the AA has to maintain and direct here can partly incorporate the most complex signal patterns in extensive sections of the cerebral cortex. In particular, extreme accomplishments are generated if this concerns patterns which represent visual or linguistic information.

Long-term memory is based on growth in synapses. A simple signal or excitation pattern does not yet normally lead to information being stored in the form of synaptic connections. This kind of information storage is based much more on repetition and assessment. If particular neuronal modules are affected by particular excitation patterns again and again, and if in the process particular chemical combinations occur, the synaptic connections grow or are altered. These connections then last longer, in extreme cases for a lifetime. The analogy to the computer is the persistent memory or the hard disk.

The Attention Assessor (AA) is largely responsible for write access in this memory. Patterns which are dominant for a time in the cerebral cortex, stimulated by the AA, are inscribed in the synaptic memory. In general the storage time of the short-term memory (under a minute) is not enough. Only patterns which oscillate in the longer-term, that is, those which are continually activated by the AA, have the opportunity to reach the synaptic memory. Here the strength, duration and number of repeats of the signal patterns largely determine how definitively storage occurs.

The concept of the Attention Assessor is meant in the sense of the focus of the neural processes on specific matters, but not in the sense of the reciprocity between attention and inattention. Either one turns towards a particular matter or one does not do this. If one does not do this, perhaps one turns to another matter, – or not, whether or not one does this is not relevant in terms of the former matter.

The system referred to as the "Attention Assessor" has quite a critical importance in the description of the principles of the neural system, which will be looked at in more detail in the following sections and chapters.

2.4 The human as a biological being

It has already been pointed out above that a particularly important difference between biological being and machines lies in the emotions. The master model and the basic prototype of the emotions is homeostasis, i. e. the self-regulation of biochemical conditions that is essential for all animate beings. Abraham H. Maslow writes in "Motivation and Personality", Chapter 2: "A Theory of Human Motivation", section "THE BASIC NEED HIERARCHY / The Physiological Needs":

> "Homeostasis refers to the body's automatic efforts to maintain a constant, normal state of the blood stream. Cannon (1932) described this process for (1) the water content of the blood, (2) salt content, (3) sugar content, (4) protein content, (5) fat content, (6) calcium content, (7) oxygen content, (8) constant hydro-

gen-ion level (acid-base balance), and (9) constant temperature of the blood. Obviously this list could be extended to include other minerals, the hormones, vitamins, and so on." (Maslow 1987, 15)

In the human brain, the corresponding functions are located in particular in the so-called hypothalamus. As the vegetative centre, this area of the brain is, together with other areas closely linked to this (such as the so-called brain stem), and together with specific glands (such as the so-called pituitary gland), responsible for combining the biochemical processes taking place in the body with the neural processes. What is fundamental here is that the processes influence each other in both directions, and that in general they are of a regulatory nature. Biochemical conditions and their alteration are converted into neural signal patterns and retransmitted. Conversely, the brain is able to influence body conditions through the release of messenger substances (as for example through hormones).

The hypothalamus is closely linked to the limbic system which, again, is the most fundamental part of the central control unit, for which the concept of Attention Assessor (AA) was introduced above. This interdependence is largely responsible for the fact that the vegetative regulatory processes are closely linked to functions like memory, evaluation/gratification, attention control and ultimately the entire signal processing in the cerebral cortex.

This narrow, basic interaction of vegetative regulatory processes with the neural processes in the (phylogenetic) oldest part of the brain, results in the fact that complying with the supply parameters is not only, as in systems engineering, an important objective, but that it is a direct core component in the basic mechanisms of action. Physiological parameters drifting off nominal values and corresponding mechanisms on their regulation are installed directly in the central control unit. This results in an important influence on the control processes, which acts via the AA on all cerebral regions.

To sum up, we can assert that the evaluation of all information processing, information storage and activity management processes through vegetative parameters is a basic principle of the brain processor.

Concepts such as feeling, sensation or emotion exist as a closer characterisation of this principle. However, here there is inevitably the realisation that these concepts involve much more than only the possibility of the perception of conditions such as hunger, thirst, shortage of breath, fever etc. However, we can assume that the basic physiological needs represent the most fundamental and most compelling part of feelings.

A further, more important, central part of the world of feelings are feelings of pain. On the one hand they form an important additional component of the vegetative-physiological interface of the brain – because from there signals are made which communicate particularly drastic faults in the body. On the other hand, there are also feelings of pain which can be released via the five senses. In both cases, signals are also then received and processed through the relevant receptors, if there is no pain. We can first talk about pain if a kind of overload occurs, i.e. if the strength of the signal exceeds a certain threshold.

The result is that the projection fields which can be assigned to the five senses in the cerebral cortex have a dual function – on the one hand they are responsible for quite normal perception, and on the other hand they are also responsible for communicating alarm signals in exceptional situations. In the latter case, the signals ultimately tend to function like vegetative signals, as evaluative control parameters, rather than as content to be processed, in which smooth transitions between the two functions can be assumed. Furthermore, there are also receptors and nerve tracts which are specialised in the fast transmission of signals representing pain.

However, in the broader sense, both functional principles – the informational and the evaluative – should be considered separately from each other. Particularly with all signals which achieve an evaluative effect in the AA, it is important to realise that their effect always occurs both gradually as well as differentially.

“Gradually” means that they have a certain intensity and that their effect is largely dependent on this.

In this regard, the concept “differential” has two meanings:

- What is essential is not the absolute value of the signal, but the gradual change which takes place while the neural information processing procedures to be evaluated are in operation.
- What is essential is not the absolute value of the signal, but the relative strength compared to all other signals operating at the same time. Here we must bear in mind that individual signals or signal currents are already subject to reinforcing or inhibiting influences on their way to the AA, so that the strength of the signal released by the receptors alone is not the only decisive factor.

2.5 *The human as a being with needs and emotions*

Besides vegetatively induced feelings and perceptions, as well as feelings of pain, which are processed as pure, distinct and compelling signals, a human being's mind is, however, usually full of diverse feelings with a less definite dominance and direction of action. Normally, it tends to be the case that the basic feelings are not active and that they leave room for a more complex and at the same time more subtle world of feelings. If, however, one of the basic needs is not satisfied, (such as, for example, that for food), then the corresponding feeling dominates the entire pursuit. In this case, the AA only works to serve feelings of hunger, and positive evaluations are only given for processes which are absolutely in the service of removing this deficit. However, as soon as this special basic need is satisfied, and if in the meantime no other need of an urgent nature has been pushed to the fore, there is once again room for higher, more subtle needs.

An interesting source on this issue is the already mentioned classic of the humanistic psychologist Abraham H. Maslow, entitled "Motivation und Personality", in which a so-called hierarchy of needs is proposed. Maslow assumes that the human psyche is shaped by a relative dominance of needs. Here higher needs can only develop if lower needs are satisfied. In addition to typical deficiency needs (such as, for example, hunger, the need for sleep and safety, etc.), at the higher level there are also growth needs, such as the need for education and self-actualisation. This concept will be looked at in more detail below.

The question here is how, in addition to homeostasis, vegetative drive and pain signals which are apparently integrated into the control of the neuronal system as a basic mode of action, more complex and more subtle feelings arise. This is the question of how emotions develop alongside and from the drives, and how both forms can interact.

In fact this can easily be explained. In principle it should be assumed here that any feelings and emotions can be attributed to basic instincts and feelings of pain.

However, how can it happen that pleasures like hearing a symphony or a metal riff, culinary pleasures, feelings which are triggered by works of art or the ascent of a mountain etc., can be attributed to basic instincts where they can only develop a long way away from any deficiency.

The answer is as follows:

Usually, for instincts and feelings of pain, the spectrum of feelings can only range from extreme deficiency (close to minus infinity) to complete calm (close to zero). However, after removing the greatest need, the experience of deficiency automatically provokes a search for the opposite (in the direction plus infinity). The neural system and, particularly, the AA, automatically maintain preventive courses of action, and the indicator for this is feelings which can represent the opposite of feelings of deficiency. An intra-neural competition for signal sequences flows from this principle, which can represent as large a distance as possible from feelings of deficiency.

At the same time, there is a complex information processing and control mechanism which, particularly via the AA, is connected to the signals that are evaluatively active, which represent gradients relating to the fulfilment of basic needs. Whatever happens with this mechanism, during or shortly before a positive gradient relating to a basic need occurs, whether this is a perception or a sensorimotor controlled action, or a signal which only circulates internally, it is registered as a positive experience in the memory. Thus at first we have arrived at the Pavlovian reflex, and we can adhere to the basic principle that the preservation of signal sequences in the cerebrum is closely connected to the respective evaluations. The feeling here is the totality of everything – the positive evaluation gradients and the information processing signal patterns in the relevant areas of the cerebral cortex. From this one can at least conclude, in relation to the basic satisfaction of needs, that there are no neural processes without evaluation and feelings. Furthermore, it follows that the cerebrum, after functioning for only a short time, is full of stored patterns, which are in principle linked with feelings. These memories can also be identified as basic experiences.

If the greatest need is satisfied then, as already indicated above, on the one hand the result is automatically a particular, also longer lasting pressure to contrast the frustration already experienced with positive experiences. On the other hand life goes on, namely the human being moves, he experiences something and it works in him – and all that is brought together with the previous memories and experiences, as far as the neural information processing mechanism allows. So in principle one can assume that a constant intensive recombination of previous memories and experiences takes place together with what has just been experienced and perceived. Here recombination also always means that the associated blends of feelings are recombined. Thus more complex information processing procedures are always inseparably linked to correspondingly complex evaluation components and feelings in the cerebral cortex.

In fact all feelings go back to basic instincts, and the stimulus also results from the corresponding experiences of deficiency. However, what can come from this through endless interconnected recombinations – and linked to new experiences – are the most complex contents, with emotions that are very far from basic feelings, which are sought as positive deficiency-distance-feelings, but which can also be experienced at any time as negative feelings of failure.

In this way, basic deficiency experiences result in a development which ultimately leads to such phenomena as aesthetic experience, sentimentality, sociability, spirituality, sport, intangible and tangible wealth. All of these are as measured by the original mechanism, homeostasis, but quite extreme phenomena result from the motivation to want to demonstrate the greatest possible distance from deficiency. Here there is the pursuit of elation, which the human being can ultimately continue to push by means of its ephemeral (differential) nature.

It should be noted that, if we again wish to consider this in a technical-mechanistic way, the term "control unit" for the AA is not quite accurate. More precisely, this is instead about a closed-loop control system in which homeostatic parameters represent setpoint values and emotions represent the corresponding divergence indicators. So phrases such as "the human being regulates his affairs", "the human being is controlled by feelings" are very compatible with the concept of the AA.

2.6 *Perception, actions and thinking*

The accomplishments of the cerebrum and the nervous system can be divided into three categories:

- Perception,
- Actions,
- Recombination.

Perception

The effect of physical and chemical parameters from the environment, or physiological parameters from one's own body, is converted by receptors into neural signals and sent on its way via afferent nerve pathways in the direction of the cerebrum. In the cerebral cortex, it reaches modules or projection fields which specialise in the direct processing of signals, specifically to the receptors which are connected to these. Furthermore, the processing of the signals proceeds via further cascades of cortical areas and modules, in which the information is just as condensed and particular features are as filtered as had proved reasonable during evolution.

On the way to the cerebral cortex, the signals normally already pass several synapses in which, on the one hand, inhibiting or exciting effects can occur, and in which, on the other hand, the signals can also already be divided between several nerve cords, which transmit the signals to different centres. In the cerebral cortex, the signals first reach the primary sensory cortical areas, which can clearly be attributed to the particular sense and body area. So there are somatosensory areas (areas for bodily feelings), visual areas (sight), auditory areas (hearing) etc.

In the visual cortex, for example, as part of the processing procedure for the signals emanating from the retina of the eye, special features are filtered out. These are, for example, brightness and colour contrasts, length, width and direction of bright lines, forms such as squares, rectangles, triangles and stars (see Popper/Eccles 2006, 264ff., Chapter E2: "Conscious perception", section 10.: "Visual perception", subsection 10.2.: "Stages in Reconstitution of the Visual Image"). In advanced processing stages "objects can be recognised independently of their apparent size" (see ibid. 270ff., subsection 10.3.: "The Perceived Visual Image").

With condensed information processing, there is also increasingly a connection of the signals of different senses. On the one hand that leads to the different senses working together, on the other hand also to redundant pathways, which lead to comparable results: "In palpation there is first the shaping of the hand for grasping an object, and secondly the moving of the hand over the surface of the object in an active exploration. In this way cutaneous sensing leads to feature detection that matches the visual feature detection in the inferotemporal lobe, as described below" (ibid. 260, Chapter E2: "Conscious Perception", section 9.: "Cutaneous Perception (Somaesthesis)", subsection 9.3.: "Secondary and Tertiary Sensory Areas").

Finally, the results of perception arrive in varied, differently compressed and abstract form in the areas of the cerebral cortex, in which they can be used in the context of control functions and in the context of recombination, also, in particular, through the AA. Here they are also basically involved in the processes which are related to evaluation and memory storage.

Actions

Active actions are closely linked to the motor areas of the cerebral cortex. Thus there are motor areas which can be quite precisely assigned to individual fingers, toes, the shoulder, the face etc. The stimuli that function there are directed to the respective muscles via efferent nerve pathways and interfaces and produce specific contractions there. An important point here is that every movement already requires a complex control and coordination mechanism.

A simple form of action control occurs, for example, through the fact that when a muscle contracts (flexor), the related antagonistic muscle (extensor) is automatically inhibited via a reflex circuit in the spinal cord. So it is clear that any control of movement can only succeed if there are responses. For this there are kinaesthetic receptors and related nerve pathways.

More complex coordination functions are carried out by the cerebellum. Thus, with pre-programmed movements, the motor modules of the cerebral cortex are relieved of the function of having to control movement in a detailed way. At the same time, however, they constantly receive information about the current status of the movement, and they can ultimately trigger other types of pre-programmed movements or – in terms of explorative movements – can at any time act in a manipulative way.

Control of movement is also always intrinsically linked to the perception of movements. In this sense, all principles which are described above for the perception mechanism are also valid for the control mechanism. Nor is perception ever a fully passive process, so that perception and control of movements are always complementary.

A special role is played by the language centre, or language centres. One of the most complex systems of the cerebrum has developed here from a combination of the processing of auditory signals and motor control of the vocal chords, which forms the essential basis for human communication and the acquisition of knowledge. This system is of course also closely linked to many other parts of the nervous system. So language is mainly used to express present perceptions and issues that are currently considered to be important. The speech process is closely linked to the processes of evaluation and attention control, which occur in the cerebrum by means of the AA, and it involves other motor processes in terms of the body language.

Recombination

All issues shall be discussed here, some aspects of which are, inter alia, described by the following expressions:

- attention control (what, how strong, how important), action control,
- short-term memory,
- thinking, awareness, self-conscious mind,
- recognition of the temporal dimension relating to sensory, sensorimotor and emotional patterns, sense of time, ability to plan,
- flexible adaptation to changed situations, ability to solve problems.

The possibility for recombination and everything that follows from this can essentially be attributed to the accomplishments of the central cerebrum processor – of the Attention Assessor (AA) set out above. In any case, it plays the decisive central role here. Which precise areas of the brain can be attributed to the AA, and which would instead be integrated as an associated performance provider, should, as far as possible, be left open here – apart from the limbic system, which must certainly be included in this.

The basic principle of the functioning of the AA consists in the fact that it has access to a large number of important areas of the cerebrum, and in this way it is able to direct their activities. At the same time, the aspect of evaluation in all brain processes is integrated through this path, which again also plays a crucial role in the process of the flexible formation of synapses, which ultimately makes long-term memory possible. Furthermore, it has already been pointed out above that an important basic principle of AA consists in the fact that, via subliminal oscillations of previous neural activity patterns, it allows simultaneous switching between different procedures.

Further important principles are as follows:

- Variability,
- Combination.

"Variability" is to be understood as the fact that the process which is dominant in the AA is subject to constant alterations. Not every flow of signals is like the previous one. In several cortex modules which are involved in the current procedure, the weight is slightly shifted, first in one direction, then in another. The activated neurons again send signals to modules that are adjacent, or which are connected to them. In this way, the AA manages to activate cortex modules via detours, to which it does not necessarily have direct access. As the cerebrum is very complex, in this sense the detour is rather the rule than the exception. In any case, the AA is able to direct processes in the cerebrum to new content through constant variations in weight.

"Combination" is to be understood as the fact that switching can not only occur between different, in fact simultaneously running, procedures, but that new combinations can be generated from the excitation patterns involved. Between different patterns, which are, as it happens, simultaneously active, a completely new, emergent pattern is compiled.

For example, it can happen that an activity that has just taken place is recombined with a memory content, which until then had no connection at all with this kind of activity. Normally, also, nothing emerges here that could have any kind of importance, or that must be evaluated positively. Sometimes, however, a spark is triggered, and a memory content from a particular context can stimulate problem-solving which has occurred in a completely different context.

In relation to the ability for the almost infinite recombination of brain processes, concerning both memory content as well as activities that have just been directed, there is also, in particular, the possibility for creating a connection between processes that occur, or that have occurred at completely different times, or that can be anticipated or proposed for future points in time. To this is added the ability for flexible adaptation to changing situations, and the ability to plan. The possibility for recombination does not necessarily lead to such accomplishments. With humans, however, this has clearly succeeded.

How can we now, in this regard, explain phenomena like thinking and awareness, and what is the connection between thinking and acting?

In principle this is quite easy, on the basis of the assumptions described above.

All the processes and excitation patterns that dominate in the cerebrum are at the same time those which the human being experiences, what he sees, hears, tastes, feels, what he thinks etc. As the AA controls the respective events, it also controls the inner experience and all activities. Caused by signals which, in a significant way, indicate threatening external influences (pain etc.), or internal deficiencies, it can be turned from current procedures to other themes, but then it continues to control events in the brain, now in the sense of new demands.

The difference between thinking and awareness, on the one hand, and action and being active, on the other hand, emerges because in principle the brain has a simulation mode. A generalisable inhibitory mechanism in a central position (i.e. a blocking mechanism) makes it possible for a substantial part of the excitation patterns to be able to pass through, both in the sense of an actual procedure and in the sense of a simulation. In the latter case, the inner experience is comparable, but the motor function is not actively controlled, at least not with the normal intensity.

Thus it is initially possible that actual activities, as well as perceptions which are also indirectly always linked to at least minimal activity, can later be experienced again and remembered, without the activity being performed again every time. This purely neuronal repetition is also possible when the body is already in a context which would no longer allow the actual process. For example, the details of a ski run can be remembered, even though one has been in a house, away from the ski slopes, for a long time.

An interesting aspect is that the simulatory blocking mechanism does indeed act in a generalised way in relation to the whole motor mechanism, but not in relation to all the procedures that are happening simultaneously. Each of the procedures is either completely blocked, or it takes place in a fully active way. So in principle something can be thought about while at the same time, in fact simultaneously, an activity can be controlled. Of course with activities the demands on neural resources are always very high, and the capacity which remains for inner experience and the variation of other sequences is limited, but in principle this is the mode of operation. Free capacity is very dependent on to what extent the operation of the activity is already automated.

Apart from the ability to simultaneously act and to think of something else, in addition the simulation mode opens up a whole world of new possibilities. Through this, recombination products can be developed which would never really be realisable. This does not mean that they would be disconnected from the sensorimotor mechanism, but they can be detached from any actual context of activity. Thus there is the possibility of adding elements to the inner experience which are completely fictitious, or which refer to contexts in the past, future, or to any far distant locations.

Thus in principle the world of human cognition has no limits. This is what constitutes thinking and awareness. In relation to language, the phenomenal development of human society as we experience it is possible. In addition, the ability of the human being, which results from recombination processes, to move in the most different contexts and to compare these to each other also leads him to encounter his ego and to have self-awareness.

Here any neural processes are not to be separated from emotions. In some cases, the emotional components are fairly weakly developed, but are never completely lacking.

We have long left behind the pathway of analogies to the computer and to automation technology, as computers know no evaluation and no past frustrations which later drive them to peak performance. Computers are much more one of many artificial extended arms which humans' AA has created – in the hope of being able to use this at any time. Without the AA they would not have developed, and without the AA of the computer user, the system administrator, the software service provider, etc., today they would also have no value.

2.7 Human speech

Human speech emerged at the intersection of a series of different accomplishments of the neural system, and requires the involvement of several areas of the cortex.

Popper and Eccles (2006) emphasise the importance of associability for the faculty of speech in Chapter E4 "The Language Centres of the Human Brain":

> "Particular importance is attached to Brodmann's areas 39 and 40, which came very late in evolution, being barely recognizable in nonhuman primates. These are the areas specifically concerned in cross-modal associations, that is associations from one sensory input, say touch, to another, say vision […]. It is postulated that language comes when you have the association between objects that you feel and objects that you see, and which you then name. […]. Language provides the means of representing objects abstractly

and for manipulating them hypothetically in one's mind." (295f.)

Further important components of the faculty of speech are areas of the brain which are related to the use of language. These include the area controlling the motor function of the vocal chords, and all areas of the cerebral cortex, which are involved in linguistic perception via eyes and ears. An especially interesting aspect is that, with one of the many possible forms of use, reading aloud, probably all the relevant areas and projection systems can be involved at once. There are also important and demanding functions here in the coding and decoding of linguistic signals.

Brodmann's areas 39 and 40, mentioned in the quotation above, belong to the most important part of the system of speech, which is called Wernicke's speech area, or the posterior speech cortex. Usually this is only in the left hemisphere of the human cortex, which Popper and Eccles also call the dominant hemisphere. Here in humans highly specialised neural structures have developed which are responsible for the fact that speech can not only be used or experienced mechanically, but also that the meaning of the particular constructs is recognised.

From the basic principle, speech is also initially based on the principles of perception, control, evaluation in the AA, and storage in the synapse memory (long-term memory), already described above. As with other specific accomplishments of the cerebrum, a decisive factor is variability and flexibility, which results from the application of the simulation and recombination principle to linguistic processing operations. To this can be added the fact that, with humans, extensive specific structures have been developed, which are a particular support for the complex accomplishments of the system of speech.

Here it should not be forgotten that it is possible for an individual human being to use speech for himself alone, – for example he can write something and read this again later, or he can think in linguistic terms. However, both in terms of evolution and also in daily existence, human society should be of fundamental importance for the use of speech. The need to provide increasingly far-reaching common achievements as an appropriate reaction to changing environmental influences may have crucially advanced the development of speech.

Through the wonder of speech, two new dimensions of possibilities were developed for neural perception and action mechanism, in particular:

- The possibility of giving expression to any actual and notional issues and to describe these in a sophisticated way, including the particular context. By consistently including further instruments – such as visual representation, literary language, data storage etc. – ultimately the possibility of using persistent (durable) ways of expression was also developed.
- The possibility of being able to share these descriptions with an, in principle, unlimited number of fellow human beings, and so to be able to develop potential on the way to awareness, which is far beyond that which would be possible for a single individual. Here it is not only collaboration in groups that is successful, but also the cooperation of human beings that are far from each other in time. In principle, the tendency that the history of the global population leads to a large, common pathway to awareness grows out of this.

The categories of thinking, awareness and the self-conscious mind can be explained in particular by the application of the faculty of the neural mechanism for memory, simulation and recombination to all those processes which are related to linguistic understanding and linguistic expression, as well as to all further typically human forms of communication. In principle, however, this is no other quality than the application of the faculty for memory, simulation and recombination to any non-communicative perception and action processes, or primitive forms of communication, for example how they also exist in mammals (body language, vocalisation etc.). Animals can think as well. Their neural world is often only slightly less rich or differently rich than that of humans.

2.8 Popper's World 3

A completely new world of the products of the human mind is established from the qualities of the human neural mechanism in relation to awareness, action and thinking, in particular in connection with the linguistic possibilities for expression – the world of stories and myths, the arts, theories, scientific discoveries, religions, spirituality etc. This world is no purely imaginary world, but it also defines itself through material objects, the formation of which develops via the human mind. These are, for example, works of art, tools, books etc. Popper und Eccles (2006) call this new world "World 3" – see especially the following sections: Chapter P1: "Materialism Transcends Itself", subsection 7.: "Nothing New Under the Sun. Reductionism and 'Downward Causation'" (14ff.); Chapter P2: "The Worlds 1, 2 and 3", subsection 11.: "The Reality of World 3" (38ff.).

This is not the place to engage in the discussion about schools of thought like materialism or dualism. There should also be no discussion about which of the concepts advanced by Popper and Eccles seem to be plausible and which are not. However, the explanations on the so-called World 3 should at least be looked at here.

It is true that this World 3 is created by the human mind, but the actions, principles and developments which control this cannot be fully deduced from their physical basis, the human body with the nervous system. World 3 has in fact taken on a life of its own in two aspects:

1. The human body was the pre-condition for access to this world being possible, but instead it is only the medium for it, in the same way that a CD is the medium for the music which is stored on it and which can be played from this. On a blank CD, it is not at all obvious which music is in the end stored on it. Neither is it determined and predictable what the human mind can create.
2. World 3 has produced results which will still exist, even if their development medium no longer does. These are once again all cultural evidence of the special human pathway to conflict with the environment. On the other hand, these are scientific laws, such as for example mathematics, physics, chemistry etc. For example, Pythagoras' theorem would also be true if it had never been discovered by a human being. Anyone facing this kind of geometry problem must also come to the same result. This is also true of natural laws which have not yet been discovered.

From this point of view, the human brain is a medium which has pushed open the door to a world without borders, which cannot be defined via this entry mechanism.

A crucial ingredient for entry to this world is emotion, which follows from the AA-based functioning of the brain processor. This is seen as an obstacle on the pathway to rational decisions. In fact, however, if necessary, human emotions neither hinder acting in a very precise way, nor managing perceptions which conform to objective criteria. For cases in which perception, motor function and intellectual faculties are not enough to reach a particular aim, the human being finds out how to create the necessary man-made resources.

With the conclusion that the world of perceptions and neural patterns, as well as the human mind and its products, is not in the least determined by the nervous system, at the same time possible objections that the assumptions made here would follow a technocratic view or a reductionist approach can be dispelled. The miracle of the soul is not lost. The scope for any assumptions and branches of science which apply to the human psyche is not affected.

2.9 The human being regulating his affairs

The preceding explanation on thinking and the self-conscious mind is mainly based on Popper and Eccles 2006. However, a few key questions are answered differently. In particular, the explanatory model is not included in the source using the concepts of the Attention Assessor (AA), simulation and recombination.

The question arises of what advantage this explanatory model of the functioning of the neural system could have. One could also simply talk about human rationality, of cognitive, planning, creative faculties, cleverness, the abilities to gain knowledge and to judge or the self-conscious mind.

The answer is: this model satisfies the actual functioning of the neural system better, and it can better explain why accomplishments and mistakes in human beings are so closely related. If the human being is not simply seen as an intelligent being but as a being who has, it is true, certain opportunities to discover and to shape his surroundings, as well as to organise coexistence in the community, but who otherwise is largely confronted by external and internal realities, then one does come slightly nearer to the truth.

The question of whether the human being has free will or not seems superfluous in this context. Both answers, yes and no, are correct. Free will is given, insofar as in the assessment process of the AA there is always a certain variability, certain opportunities which can be alternated between, and which therefore always provide scope for decision-making. Free will is not given, insofar as the needs are incorporated into the assessment process as the crucial reference variable, and so in principle there is no escape from its imperative nature.

The latter circumstance ensures that usually the human being cannot simply follow the rules of a down-to-earth, rational reason. It also ensures that different individuals do have similar, in part even the same, maxims for their actions, but that normally this is at different times, in different contexts, with different orientations for the goals, so that social conflicts are pre-programmed. Even when the goals, for whatever reason, are aligned with each other, this again favours the development of resource shortage and thus produces further cause for conflict.

However, the good news is that there are always alternatives and an almost infinite scope for creative ways out of any problems and dilemmas. The key to this is the desire to use the AA. In the most basic case this works, in the immediate context of a recombination or thought process, by looking for possible alternatives. However, the possibilities are on the whole much greater. Because the way is always open to mentally transcend this horizon, to intellectually trawl through memories and experiences, to seek fictions and assumptions, to widen or restrict the view in terms of space, time or society.

Thus the image of the human being represented here can also be summarised by the following phrase:

The human being is a creature who regulates his affairs.

One can also say on this that:

To regulate his affairs, the human being has excellent and at the same time very complex abilities. These abilities allow him to look far beyond the context of immediate interaction with his environment by creating and recombining images of a multitude of contexts in the nervous system. Of crucial importance is also the ability to look beyond one's own individual existence, and to be able to operate successfully in social conditions. This results in a tendency for the variety of objective problems, to which the human being was once originally subject, to be increasingly relocated in the subjective world of the imagination. This explains the growing risk that the human being could primarily fail due to problems of the internal world that are reproduced in the neural system, the relevant social interactions and the products of the human mind, rather than due to external, objective circumstances.

In this regard, Popper/Eccles (2006) wrote in Chapter P6: "Summary" (209f.):

> "(9) Natural selection, and selection pressure, are usually thought of as the results of a more or less vio-

> lent struggle for life.
>
> But with the emergence of mind, of World 3, and of theories, this changes. We may let our theories fight it out – we may let our theories die in our stead."

But this is in no way solely about theories but mostly about much more mundane matters. In any case, the possibility that in principle exists, to largely avoid physical death through deliberate and clever behaviour, is not always used.

What is included when man manages his affairs can be discussed very well using Maslow's hierarchy of needs.

2.10 Maslow's hierarchy of needs

From the principles described above of vegetative needs and emotions, it is already clear that in the neural system, on the one hand, lower needs with a relatively clear orientation, and on the other hand, higher needs with complex and ambivalent consistence, are of great importance. The functioning of the neural system is decisively characterised both by basic needs and more complex emotions. Here lower needs can, if they are not then satisfied, function in a markedly dominant way, and as far as possible take over the neural mechanism. If lower needs are satisfied, there is room for higher needs to appear, where the emotions do in fact also go back to a mixture of experiences of shortage, but where the opposite is usually pursued – e.g. as experience of elation or abundance.

The humanistic psychologist Maslow (1987) writes in "Motivation and Personality", Chapter 2: "A Theory of Human Motivation", section "THE BASIC NEED HIERARCHY":

"But what happens to their desires when there *is* plenty of bread and when their bellies are chronically filled? [...] *At once other (and higher) needs emerge* and these, rather than physiological hungers, dominate the organism. And when these in turn are satisfied, again new (and still higher) needs emerge, and so on. This is what we mean by saying that the basic human needs are organized into a hierarchy of relative prepotency." (17)

In addition to the physiological basic needs, Maslow also refers, amongst others, to the following types of needs, from low to high:

- Need for safety,
- Need for belonging and love,
- Need for esteem,
- Need for self-actualisation, the demand for knowledge and understanding, aesthetic needs.

There is a summary in the following table (higher needs are at the top, needs which can become prepotent are at the bottom):

Table 1 – The hierarchy of needs (based on Abraham H. Maslow)

Category of needs	**Examples of respective needs**
Need for culture and self-actualisation, need for growth (Level 5)	A need to be able to do in social life what the single human being is suited for as an individual: "Musicians must make music, artists must paint, poets must write if they are to be ultimately at peace with themselves" (Maslow 1987, 22); A need to live in the middle of society, and thus

Category of needs	**Examples of respective needs**
	at the same time to be able to remain true to one's own, quite individual, nature; curiosity, the demand for knowledge and understanding; the ambition to be driven by the urge for mental growth, instead of only by shortage needs.
Need for esteem and recognition/individual needs (level 4)	Need for esteem, self-esteem, strength, achievement, accomplishment and skills, a good reputation, prestige, status, fame, recognition, attention, importance, dignity, appreciation
Need for belonging and love, social needs (level 3)	Need for a place in a group, for belonging to a family, for friendship, for a loving relationship, for avoiding loneliness, ostracism, rejection, isolation, dislocation
Need for safety (level 2)	Safety, stability, security, protection, freedom from fear; need for structure, order, law, boundaries
Basic physiological needs (level 1)	Homeostatic needs (in particular affecting blood parameters) such as hunger, thirst, the need to breathe; sexual desire, sleep, need for movement or activity, need to be free from pain

Maslow points out that it is difficult and at the same time not very sensible to want to draw up a comprehensive catalogue of needs. Also, it is difficult to definitely allocate a need to a category. The needs and their satisfaction must be seen much more as a very complex process:

"It should be pointed out again that any of the physiological needs and the consummatory behavior involved with them serve as channels for all sorts of other needs as well. That is to say, the person who thinks he or she is hungry may actually be seeking more for comfort, or dependence, than for vitamins or proteins. Conversely, it is possible to satisfy the hunger need in part by other activities such as drinking water or smoking cigarettes. In other words, relatively isolable as these physiological needs are, they are not completely so." (Maslow 1987, 16)

Maslow also gives important advice regarding the "Degrees of Satisfaction" (ibid., 27): lower needs must not necessarily be one hundred per cent satisfied for each of the higher needs to become more important.

Human beings whose basic needs were largely satisfied in the past also endure temporary frustrations better; in this regard, the concept of gratification health is used. It should also be noted that needs are often processed unconsciously, that they are dependent on culture, and that thinking and acting are usually determined by multiple motivations.

The hierarchy of needs is often illustrated as a *pyramid* of needs. The tiers or levels must be seen in such a way that the lower levels each have a more basic importance than each of those above. Level 1 is the basis for all other levels. It has the most fundamental importance. It can also be described as taking up the largest area. Level 2 builds on this and again forms the basis for all the other levels.

The attribute "pyramid" also means that the higher levels can be temporarily or permanently meaningless, if an emergency occurs at one of the lower levels. The lower levels are each fall-back levels for the levels lying above them. In the event of the worst disaster, only level 1 still counts, in which it is about naked survival. This simple mechanism corresponds to Maslow's statement "that the basic human needs are organized into a hierarchy of relative prepotency." (Maslow 1987, 17)

However the needs and their effect are defined – the principle of needs and their frustration or fulfilment is a further approach to describe the processes which were explained above as the principle of differential assessment in the human AA, and as the principle of emotion. With all these perceptions, the rule is also, in particular, that more basic needs and emotions are more prone to unambiguousness and dominance – if they then become active –, while higher needs and emotions are characterised more by complexity. Overall this is about endowing the neural system with a wide range of useable patterns. The claim here is that a system of patterns is formed that not only contains strategies which can secure naked survival, but also those which are able to equip the individual with a certain degree of vitality. Vitality in the sense of the neural system is to be understood as the greatest possible distance from any feeling of shortage and frustration. It is realised in the form of elation and aesthetic experiences.

The hierarchy of needs has meanwhile become the subject of many subsequent and also critical observations, and the question is also partly posed of to what extent Maslow's model, which originated in 1954, can still be regarded as valid today. Moreover, Maslow himself later made observations, which are not considered here. In this regard, what is important is above all to take note of the principle of the changing prepotency of the needs, and basically to understand that they are organised in a motivation system with levels of elevation and fall-back.

In contrast, how the levels and the need categories are divided exactly is less crucial and, moreover, – as stated – culturally dependent.

In the following section as well, it depends firstly on the defined principle of division, and only then on the assignment of need categories to the respective sides and levels.

2.11 Material and aesthetic side of the world of human needs

If we take the fact that the processes in the brain are widely affected by emotions, and the hierarchy of needs as a given, the question remains: why are property and consumption, that is, "material" values, able to play such a prominent role in today's society? Of course, the human being is made of matter, he lives in an environment which is made of matter and he interacts with it. Human behaviour is a reaction to processes in the environment and it has an influence on this environment. But that is only one aspect of human existence. A full picture can only appear if the internal world is included in considerations. Then the result is that neural and environmental procedures are two sides of the same coin, which depend on one another.

The following table shows a variant of the hierarchy of needs, which considers this duality.

Table 2 – Hierarchy of needs with aesthetic and material aspects

B – Aesthetic aspect	**A** – Material aspect
5 – Culture/self-actualization/growth	
Need to constantly develop one's capabilities and talents, need for knowledge and understanding, need to be able to go one's own way in the social environment; need to make a positive contribution to the welfare of fellow human beings, the development of human society, environmental protection; religious and spiritual needs; need for culture and, perhaps, for enlightenment	Sufficient material basics for culture and self-actualization, material riches
4 – Individual needs/esteem need	
Esteem, reputation, prestige, recognition (awards, praise), influence, personal and professional achievement, mental and physical strength, stable self-esteem	Material prosperity; financial means, tangible assets, fashion, consumption – for personal use and to symbolise status and prestige
3 – Belongingness needs/social needs	
Family, friends, partnership, love, intimacy, communication, social integration and cohesion, belonging to a	Sufficient material basics to be able to maintain family ties, friendship, partnership and all other kinds of social

B – Aesthetic aspect	**A** – Material aspect
community	relationships and social integration
2 – Safety needs	
Feeling of safety and physical integrity; no fear and anxiety; legal certainty is guaranteed; need for structure	Safety, stability, law and order; protection against danger; fixed minimum living wage; safer accommodation
1 – Physiological needs/homeostasis	
Hunger, thirst; need to breathe, sleep, sexuality, exercise and activity; temperature balance, homeostatic balance	Food, water, fresh air; sufficient possibilities for sleeping, sex, exercise and activity; beneficial surrounding temperature, sufficient preconditions for complying with homeostatic regulation

Maslow classified the demand for self-actualisation as a special phenomenon, observable with some human beings. But here we will go a step further. The assumption is that a healthy, fit human has a collection of demands at each level of the hierarchy, and it is this multiplicity of needs which determines the behaviour of the individual and social relationships, to a great extent. Deficiencies can also only be sufficiently analysed by starting from an ideal and looking for what is missing. Often the opposite approach is used – analysing pathological occurrences or carrying out animal experiments and drawing conclusions on the healthy human, which can in fact only be a comparatively provisional alternative strategy.

But the most important question regarding the dual hierarchy of needs is this of the dependencies between the two aspects. The answer is as follows:

The aesthetic aspect B is the aim, but it is based on the material aspect A. Material factors are always preconditions for the satisfaction of needs. Thus food must be available so that hunger can be satisfied. But conversely

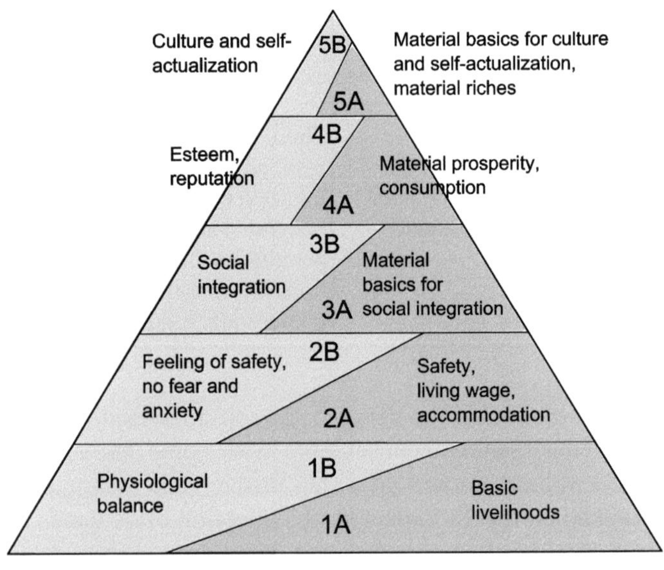

Figure 1 – Pyramid of needs

it is not completely certain that hunger will be satisfied if food is available – it must still be consumed. In relation to phenomena like esteem or self-actualisation, the aesthetic experience is also the real aim, and social, physical, monetary factors operate as pre-requisites and constraints. The human being always tries, as part of his efforts, to improve the constraints, but in the end, achieving this happens as an aesthetic experience.

Assuming that the described relationship between the material and the aesthetic side can be proven to be appropriate for all levels, an interlocked pyramid of needs might be the result, as shown in figure 1.

If we start from the assumption that this interpretation of the pyramid of needs is basically correct and that it is a reasonable description of a way of life which is widely determined by areas of need, it is reasonable to infer a few conclusions for human society. It is particularly obvious to consider current social conventions, value systems and exchange processes, as well as their dynamic, in the light of this model. The following chapters will also address the question of how to define the healthy condition of humans, groups, society and of mankind as a whole, how could it be approached, and what are the obstacles in the way.

2.12 Pyramid of needs and vitality system

Up to now the focus has been on a few special aspects of the functioning of the neural system. We can summarise the result along these lines:

- The functioning of the neural system is based on forwarded electro-chemical excitation patterns which constantly circulate in it and which are affected by receptor signals, reflecting external parameters or events.
- The circulation of the excitation patterns is controlled and assessed by some areas located in the central nervous system (through the Attention As-

sessor or AA). This process involves both control of the varying attention to excitation patterns and involved areas of the brain, as well as the assessment of the pattern itself. The question of which of the excitation procedures receive particularly intensive attention and special assessment ultimately decides on their inscription into the synapse store, so into the long-term memory.

- The system called the AA controls both active behaviour and active perception and exploration, as well as all the processes that take place in a simulated way. A basic principle of the functioning of the AA is that, as a general rule, several procedures are controlled simultaneously. These vary constantly, and the recombination that is possible at any time offers unlimited creative potential.
- The decisive reference for the control process (or the regulation process) is given in the form of emotion. All emotions go back to homeostatically-induced assessment processes. So-called basic experiences are formed through the homeostatic procedures, which are controlled by the AA and are therefore able to capture a significant share of the processes in the nervous system. All more complex emotions are based on these basic experiences. As all processes in the cerebrum involve the regulating and controlling effect of the AA, any memory content and any procedures are absolutely linked to an emotional element. The emotional assessment is a basic principle of the functioning of the brain.
- The different categories and levels of complexity regarding the processes in the cerebrum can be described by the definition of needs. The importance

> of different needs fluctuates, depending on the particular level of the deficiency or fulfilment. Thus the human being is controlled by the constantly changing dominance of quite different needs.

Hence there are a couple of assumptions which explain the functioning of the neural system and action. However, this does not yet sufficiently explain the question of how the human system integrates overall as an intelligent being in the processes of its environment.

When clarifying this question, we can consider the conflict which exists between the individual who regulates his means of existence and the indifferent attitude which the environment and the cosmos have towards this aspiration. The human individual's course of development can be regarded as the continuing process of climbing the pyramid of needs. However, the indifferent attitude of the cosmos causes the basis for satisfying this demand to be constantly eroded. So the human being is confronted by an environment which constantly and systematically opposes his existence to some extent.

With the neural system the human being does, however, have an instrument which shows all characteristics, in order to be able to defend the human's demands just as systematically. So individual needs are in fact, on the one hand, in competition with each other due to the fact of their changing prepotency. On the other hand, however, through the functioning of the AA and its ability to establish connections between all processes, an element comes into play which can work very well in a coordinating way. So in this way, in principle, there is the ability for reasonable and strategic action.

The human being's action as an intelligent being is realised here on several different levels. It is realised in the form of traces which are left behind in one's own nervous system, as well as in the form of traces which are left behind in the environment. Of particular quality here are the interpersonal communication processes and the processes of cooperation within society. Furthermore, existence is largely determined by those elements in the cosmos, the environment and society which are beyond any influence. So successful strategies depend essentially on whether and how successfully to coordinate perception and impact on the environment in such a way that, in terms of one's own existence, the largest synergetic effect can be achieved, combined with the conditions that cannot be directly influenced.

The human being only then has a chance if he acts in a coordinated and strategic way at all these levels. This does not mean that he has to constantly think and act strategically. However, it is about clarifying how he behaves if he has to make an effort in relation to satisfying needs and climbing the pyramid of needs. It must be regarded as probable that systematic approaches are more likely to be encountered the larger the area of conflict between demand and reality and the larger the balancing act which must be undertaken here.

This can be expressed in such a way that normally the human being is continually engaged in building something, while the environment constantly works against this ambition in a destructive way. But what is it that the human individual constructs, in what does this constructive process consist?

The concept of the "individual vitality system" should now be introduced here, with the convention of speech that the path to climbing the pyramid of needs consists of the human being constructing a vitality system and constantly reorganising and optimising it as a reaction to the natural trend towards erosion.

The concept of the vitality system assumes a connection with the concept of a healthy vitality and life force. It is true that the concept of vitality is already beset by different meanings. Regardless of these variations in interpretation, all elements which the human being constructs in terms of maintaining and easing his existence should be combined here under the concept of "vitality system".

Health is a basic element here, of course, but a few other categories should also be considered. They already follow from the hierarchy of needs:

- Body, health and fitness.
- All the potential that has accumulated in the nervous system, such as mental, psychic, artistic, emotional, intelligent potential, experiences, knowledge components, abilities etc.
- The relevant part of the social environment and all the traces that are left behind there in the context of actions and exchange processes, if here it is assumed that these traces can, if possible, be attributed to the initiator (that is, if they are not anonymous).
- The relevant part of the environment and the apparently relevant traces which are left behind in this area.
- The question of one's material circumstances, all monetary assets and liabilities, ownership, poverty/wealth, business relationships.

There is a particular situation at the adolescent stage. During child development, the vitality system is subject to a particularly substantial dynamic. The tendency towards building a system of vitality components, which correspond to the respective age group-related demands, is confronted by the constant tendency to destroy this system by the demands of the next stage in child development. This process only slows down in the context of the socialisation of the adult personality, and becomes an apparent form of the vitality system. It is only in this regard that this system achieves a certain resilience whereas, until then, it required the protection of fellow adult human beings, present in the social environment.

Conditions of deficiency, which were formative during early childhood but also during developments in childhood and adolescence, can lead to lasting damage concerning mental vitality. Here the issue of gratification health, mentioned above, is of prominent importance. In this phase, the experience that needs are satisfied is the basis for the fact that so-called basic trust can be triggered which can later be the foundation for intense tolerance of frustration, and the ability to temporarily survive deprivation without more substantial damage. If in this way crucial development stages, which there are in particular in childhood and adolescence, are shaped by corresponding deeper frustrations, there could be consequences from this which are later overcome only with great difficulty or not at all. It is precisely this which favours destructive developments.

In this sense, there is destructiveness in particular:

- if there is resignation, that is, if attitudes arise which partly or overall make climbing the pyramid of needs no longer a sensible motivation or
- if the performance development of the neural and the physiological system in the crucial ontogenetic development phases (of the individual) is affected

in such a way that later the result is objective disadvantages to abilities.

In relation to the demand to climb the pyramid of needs, the case of destructiveness is always then given:

- if parts of the vitality system of an individual collapse and cannot adequately be replaced by new constructs or
- if the socialisation of subsequent generations does not lead to the level of sufficiency of the vitality system attaining that of the parents' generation.

In relation to the last point, the differential nature of the assessment mechanism in the AA should still be considered. Stimulus arises through difference. The greater the difference between a frustration, a negative experience, a negative emotion, and the hoped for contrary elation, the higher the stimulus. Thus in addition to the experience of needs being satisfied, the experience that satisfying these is not self-evident is just as important. It is no use if children are spoiled. They must also be allowed to have the experience that not everything is self-evident, and that there is something that first needs to be fought for. The lack of this component can also lead to destructive results, as well as lasting frustrations.

2.13 The principle of differential aesthetics

Overall, the system of needs follows a principle that shall here be called the "Aesthetics Principle", or more precisely it shall be called the "principle of differential aesthetics". According to the Aesthetics Principle, individuals aspire to the most comprehensive satisfaction of needs possible, accompanied by feelings of elation; limitations can therefore be caused by the fact that climbing the pyramid of needs is not yet completely successful or that there is a case of destructiveness.

Before the Aesthetics Principle is explained in more detail, first we have to clarify what should be understood by aesthetics in this regard. The aesthetics concept is already beset by a range of meanings, which can seem to make it questionable to use it here in the sense of a principle of the world of needs. On the other hand it can hardly be avoided, if observations on human ambitions are to be made.

Aesthetics is first of all the doctrine of beauty, particularly beautiful art (see Kant's "Critique of [aesthetic] Judgement"). Primarily, the perception of harmony and beauty, – of works of art, but also of nature – is considered to be aesthetic. In a broader sense, though, aestheticism and good behaviour are also called aesthetic. Since the 19th century there have been numerous aesthetic theories. The subtleties that have been established in this regard should not be examined here. Differently than usual, the aesthetics concept shall be used much more in a generalised meaning – in the sense of a framework which allows all variations and interpretations of aesthetics.

What is aesthetics?

- Every good feeling is aesthetic.
- Every emotion has an aesthetic value, either in the positive or the negative sense.

Until now particularly complex emotions, e.g. those emotions or feelings of beauty within the perception of art, were assigned an aesthetic value. However, this is rather a reduced perception. If one accepts the assumption that – as described above – from the lowest basic need to complex intellectual or artistic processes – there is a continuity in the brain and that the internal assessment experience can be identified at every level of the pyramid of needs as emotion, then it is only logically consistent if the aesthetics concept also includes all these levels.

This is also therefore basically plausible because the more or less profoundly subtle neural processes which enable art – such as for example a classical concert – to be experienced are only possible if there are no temporary deficiencies at the lower levels of need. The satisfaction of lower needs and thereby their temporary non-dominance is therefore usually an implicit element in more complex aesthetic experiences. At the same time, art basically plays on the whole spectrum of needs and emotions – one thinks, for example, of the painting "The Meal (Still Life with Bananas)" by Paul Gauguin.

What is aesthetics, in detail? Here are a few randomly compiled examples for concepts which can express aesthetic circumstances:

> Mind, psychological wellbeing, mental wellbeing, moral values, perception precision, subtlety, sensitivity, mental strength, imagination, ability, strength, ethics, spirituality, the beauty of nature, the beauty of art, the beauty of thought and action, sentimentality, knowledge (need: curiosity), understanding, humanity/altruism, professional ethics, reputation, dignity, esteem, awe, belief, trust, not to be credulous, basic fulfilment of needs, good behaviour, non-conformance, independence, love, to be loved, sociability, pleasure, to be happy, fun, humour, sport, play.

Some of the concepts conflict with each other, or at least indicate an area of conflict. Thus sensitivity conflicts with mental strength – both are simultaneously possible, that is, in the same person at the same time, but not really in an extreme form. There are further areas of conflict between ability and strength, good behaviour and non-conformance, humanity and independence.

On the one hand, aesthetics is a comprehensive, generalisable principle, however, on the other hand, it is also contradictory and diverse. There cannot be aesthetics per se which someone defines and which all other fellow human beings can follow. Tastes are different. Aesthetics is infinite. Thus, just as the neural system has pushed open the door to World 3, to a world with endless possibilities which cannot be deduced from the development medium, the brain processor, there are also endless possibilities to define aesthetics. Aesthetics is not dogma. In the world of aesthetics, there is no standard currency. The perception of the aesthetic is always carried out by the whole person, with all his experiences and memory content. As the life story of the individual human being takes place individually, in general the process of perception always takes place in a highly complex and unique projection space.

However, aesthetics can be partially communicated. Imparting aesthetic perception is an important content of human communication (cf. also the statements on "Explanation of art and understanding of art" in Majetschak 2010, 162ff.).

A simple example, long-known and much-quoted, illustrates this. In the following picture one may either see nothing at all, or it can be seen "as the head of a rabbit or a duck" (Majetschak 2010, 164), depending on which aspect may be noticed, or which aspect should be highlighted.

Figure 2 – R-D-Head[4]

Whether both kinds of interpretation can be understood depends on different factors. There are good preconditions if the brain, in which the perception of the picture is processed, was already once involved with the perception of a living rabbit or duck. This is not self-evident for all places in the world and in the future it will be, if anything, still less self-evident than today. A further condition is a to a certain extent trained ability towards abstraction. Without already knowing about other examples of the abstract, symbolic representation of real objects or subjects, it is perhaps difficult to be able to also draw the parallels from this picture. If the conditions mentioned are absent, this may possibly be offset by the transfer of knowledge. But even if experience or knowledge exist it must, moreover, still appear sensible to engage in the respective types of interpretation. At any time the Attention Assessor has the possibility not to do this. Here, in particular, the context in which the encounter with the picture and the relevant explanations takes place also plays a crucial role.

The aesthetic world of humans is characterised by the fact that, at the intersection of any individual with his

[4] Source: Joseph Jastrow, "Fact and Fable in Psychology" (1901), taken from Majetschak 2010, 164.

social and natural environment, something quite new, unique, unprecedented and never recurring develops. In each unique context, the continuous reflection of the previous experiences and actions of fellow human beings, and in incidents in nature, takes place. In this regard as well, life is also therefore characterised by incessant creativity and emergence – not least the process of evolution as a whole.

So much for the generalised aesthetics concept. Now more detail about the Aesthetics Principle.

A possible definition of the "principle of differential aesthetics" is as follows:

- Aesthetics is the universal fulfilment principle of the neural system.
- Thus it is, moreover, also the universal fulfilment principle of the human's system of needs, as well as his individual and social existence.

In order to obtain a more precise understanding of the Aesthetics Principle, other aspects should be considered. However, all these could be logically deduced from the formula used above, as well as from the explanations which were made in the preceding sections of this chapter.

To what extent is the Aesthetics Principle to be described as "differential"?

Here the differential function of the central processor of the neural system, called the Attention Assessor (AA), should be considered, as described in sections 2.4, 2.5 and 2.10. Stimulus and motivations always only occur through an area of conflict between neural signals indicating unsatisfactory conditions or difficult living conditions and the opposing feelings of fulfilment and elation.

There are important consequences from this:

- Fulfilment can always only be a transient experience; if it is achieved, it has already begun to disappear.
- A pure principle of happiness, constantly floating in elation, is never possible. Existence is not possible without downsides and low points. If a bad situation is really successfully eliminated, then a new irritation takes its place, objectively perhaps less bad, but after a short period of familiarisation, if anything it is perceived as being equally drastic.
- The degree to which the fulfilment of a need can be experienced depends on how deep the valley is that had to be traversed before. With sporting activity, for example, the elation that can be achieved can be all the more impressive the higher the risk involved. With socially organised activities, one's own salvation and reputation is all the more earned, the worse the distress or injustice one is facing, and the more one has achieved in this regard, the higher the burden was that one had taken on.
- Without considerable burdens and risks there is no prospect of profound fulfilment. Conversely, however, complete success rarely comes from good intentions and if it does, then it is often hard to secure. Through its differential nature, then, the Aesthetics Principle largely produces the opposite condition to that which one would have hoped, namely endlessly dealing with concerns that can release unaesthetic feelings and frustrations. However, in fact fulfilment as a ubiquitous objective tends to be rather like a shy deer that is rarely seen.

- This kind of differential dynamic can only be managed by occasionally experiencing success, fulfilment, happiness, elation and, in the meantime, by trust and optimism not being lost. The prevailing mood usually experienced by every human being in this process may – depending on temperament and living conditions – be different; the mechanisms are, however, always the same.

What follows from the Aesthetics Principle in relation to the system of needs and its aesthetic and material aspect?

In section 2.11 it was established that the aesthetic aspect of the system of needs always takes precedence. The material aspect does in fact provide important conditions, but fulfilment always takes the form of an aesthetic experience. From this it follows that implicitly the Aesthetics Principle is also the fulfilment principle of the material-monetary sphere of the system of needs. When we stated above that the Aesthetics Principle is the universal fulfilment principle, this is therefore also absolutely true of the basic material conditions of life, of the economy etc. However, we are talking here not about an idealistic principle, but much more about a dualistic principle in which aesthetic ambition does in fact generally contain guidance on the direction, but where the material conditions, as well as conditions in the social and natural environment, always form the unalienable reality against which ambition has to prove itself.

Considering the ambition of the human being and of society in this way, one can regard the principle of the precedence of the aesthetic over the material sphere of the system of needs as a natural law, the infringement of which has consequences. Here it is just as much about the precedence of the Attention Assessor as a regulating authority or, in other words, about the precedence of reason, ethical competence etc., over basic material conditions and economic processes.

The question arises of whether, in the aesthetic sphere of social exchange processes, there are also market mechanisms and currencies.

In principle this is how it can be seen, but not without fully abandoning the usual criteria from material thinking. If there is a market in the aesthetic sphere then it could be a market of ideas, attitudes, interpretations, works etc. And if there is a currency in this sphere, then it could be that of attention, appreciation or reputation. There is more on this in section 3.11"The cultural currency system".

What follows from the principle of differential aesthetics?

There are many alternative approaches when considering the theme examined in this chapter, and it is the subject of many fields and research projects. It is therefore doubtful whether the theses presented here on the relationship between the neural system, the system of needs and aesthetic ambitions, are also needed. However, if one admits this view, then the Aesthetics Principle is of the utmost significance for human and society. In this case one can say, in short, that the Aesthetics Principle rules the world – what is meant is the world of human society or the whole of Popper's Worlds 2 and 3.

Here, amongst other things, the concern is also artistic aesthetics, elitist aesthetics, good behaviour, higher demands etc.; mainly, though, it is about the aesthetics of everyday life in all its aspects. Every activity of a human being has its own aesthetic and tastes are different, but also communicable. Detached forms of aesthetics are rather a side issue in society, and here they should on no account be more of a focus than they deserve.

The chapter "Culture or disaster?" showed that the current stage of development of human society is still characterised by some disastrous states. Thus it cannot be appropriate for the discourse to be continued here directly in the sense of a qualitatively high demand for aesthetics. First, it must be much more about removing serious deficiencies, which are currently to be deplored across the globe, and which can only be seen as untenable conditions, precisely because of aesthetic perceptions.

If, furthermore, we are talking about the, or one, aesthetic perception, and if particular conclusions and demands can be inferred from this, then of course this can only mean the subjective aesthetic perception of the author. This can then be seen in detail as comprehensible, and if possible it can be shared – or also not.

First the following chapter will examine a few aspects and principles which play a particular role in human society in relation to the neural system, the Aesthetics Principle and the deficiencies of current global development. Subsequently, we will look again at the different subjects of disaster, with respective conclusions and ideas for solutions.

3 The mankind organism

3.1 Needs and human society

If the pyramid of needs as a model for the satisfaction of individual needs can be described as appropriate, it must therefore also be extremely important for social life. This arises from the fact that, as already mentioned above, many needs involve interaction with society. The whole of social life, from culture and art, politics, the economy, science, education, social systems and welfare, law and order, to the question of the forms of society, is characterised by attitudes and discussions on positions in the pyramid of needs. Not only for individual humans, but also for groups, peoples and for humanity as a whole, the categories of needs mentioned and their relationships constitute an important dimension in which relationships and processes can be described and characterised.

In any kind of community there is some common denominator, there is a particular intersection of common interests, and there are goals which are followed together. If one looks for a generic concept for the common foundation that is systematically established here, then there is the "social vitality system". One can talk about the social vitality system in relation to every form of community organisation. Whether it is a family or a friendship, a sports club, a party, a democratic political system, a company, a market-based system with corresponding rules, a scientific establishment, a cultural organisation, a charitable organisation, a currency system, a clique, a criminal organisation, a Mafia organisation etc. – in each case rules are defined (casually or systematically) which result in the creation of an overlap for the individual vitality systems of the people involved. As long as it succeeds in this way in securing synergies and benefits for a substantial part of these people and their individual vitality systems, then there is a basis for the stability of the community.

Human history is characterised by a never-ending attempt to successfully climb the pyramid of needs at community level. At any time and everywhere, people are engaged in organising successful social cooperation. However, just as comprehensive is also the story of the signs of decay. Time and again friendships and families drift apart, organisations collapse, companies become bankrupt, states, currency systems and markets get into crisis situations, conflicts escalate and wars are fought. Again and again there is evidence of really destructive developments in relation to social vitality systems.

There are two particular reasons for this. First of all, a key factor lies in the dynamic of social processes, with the question of how well citizens succeed in combining their individual vitality systems with each other and with social vitality systems into a synergetic network. However, it is never possible to achieve a status in which all members benefit to the same extent, and so, even in the best of times, social development is always facing destructive activities. Thus there is constant flux between build-up and collapse. Here at any moment there is the danger that destructive potential is mutually reinforcing. So at any time there is the risk that in areas in which previously cooperation and communication have prevailed, gradually obstacles and walls emerge, and the result is the cumulative avalanche-like destruction of vitality system elements, and therefore crises and wars. In this way, collapses can happen for no obvious reasons, just as happens with freak waves in the ocean or with congestion on the motorway.

Second, every form of community is also subject to external constraints, and these are subject to constant changes. Just as the individual can be more or less successful in adapting to the dynamic inherent in the living environment and in influencing it, this is also true of the community. Therefore circumstances can arise which result in the foundation on which social agreement is based also being destroyed. Examples of such actions are shortages of resources, epidemics or environmental catastrophes. On the one hand, such changes in basic conditions happen by chance, due to the laws of nature, on the other hand, however, they can also follow from man's unsuitable actions.

In every form of crisis, the real problem lies in man's reaction to the particular situation. Just as the individual can manage to successfully overcome deprivation on the basis of gratification health and basic trust, it is important for the community that a significant part of its members should not lose the belief that problems are solvable. Only when this is no longer successful is disaster provoked.

3.2 The mankind organism

Climbing the pyramid of needs as a social process implies a continuous rise in joint participation over the course of human history. Amongst other things, our age is characterised by scientific-technical revolution, modern travel and telecommunication services, the globalised demand of the market economy, and the population explosion. All this increasingly leads to the requirement to think in global dimensions. Wellbeing, especially in the western world, seems to be dependent on steady economic growth and the increasing consumption of resources. Extrapolating trends in the western way of life and its tendency to want to export this to as many countries as possible, together with the explosive growth in the world population, may lead to the conclusion that we will run into a difficult situation. There is the threat of an extreme shortage of some resources worldwide. A self-induced global disaster might only be prevented by new approaches to finding solutions which are completely unknown, apart for a certain awareness that radical measures are necessary, which must be taken at global level. If we consider the poor ability of humans to deal with conflicts, as demonstrated by history and by the present, one could conclude that the situation is almost hopeless.

These circumstances suggest the conclusion that mankind has already long become a unified whole – a kind of huge organism. For this mankind organism the principle is also valid that it aspires to climb the pyramid of needs.

Until now this demand has obviously been accompanied by a strong ambivalence. There are extreme imbalances and internal conflicts (inside the mankind organism) and the whole system always risks collapsing into a world war or a major ecological disaster. But it is necessary to escape from the disastrous perception which results from analysing these dangers. Of course, we can and must learn from the mistakes of history. But it is much more important to develop a view of the healthy condition of the mankind organism, and about the potential in this direction. Consequently, it might be possible to investigate which elements and characteristics are still missing, and what can and must be done if possible to approach the healthy condition.

Though it would not be wise to dismiss the assumption of a healthy, fit, harmonic condition of global human society as a utopia. Instead it is sensible to see the respective assumptions as defined by a reference state, which should be aspired to and which can be partially achieved.

What are the main characteristics of the healthy, fit state of mankind?

- Every human being in the world has the chance to be involved in society by seeking satisfaction for his needs at all levels of the pyramid of needs in a well-balanced manner.
- Society tries to find ways and means for solutions, if important pre-conditions for these are not provided under special circumstances. This is done by the involvement of affected citizens and their legitimate right of sovereignty.
- Decisions about the type and priority of needs can only be done by each individual on his/her own. This is the inescapable conclusion of the emergent nature of the neural system, and the fact that in everyone's mind perceptions are unique.
- Conflicts are managed as subtly and at as high a level as possible – for more details see the chapter "The trend towards subtlety".

This definition can only be regarded as an initial, quite abstract attempt to define a reference state, in the sense of considering the pyramid of needs for the mankind organism. It can further only be understood as a supplement to previous achievements and humanistic agreements like the Universal Declaration of Human Rights, the achievements of the European Enlightenment, the rules and constitutional guarantees of democratic states, law and order, as well as all other value systems and ethical standards.

3.3 *The trend towards coalescence*

The previous section suggested that mankind has become a complete whole. It should be added that the historical development which is in fact going in this direction is at least still in full swing. In the past, the development of human society was characterised by communities initially being established within narrow borders. Groups, once formed, were dispersed across broad landscapes and continents, and had only occasional points of contact, if they had any at all. Only after a very long period of development was there also an accelerated process of coalescence in relation to scientific-technical progress and the accelerated growth in the global population. Today one can state that almost all places and countries in the world are at least informationally present in almost all other places. Interdependencies on trade routes, monetary relations, globally oriented companies, wars, environmental damage, disasters, tourism, globalisation etc. are already very widespread and are intensifying more and more. In this perspective, coalescence is a reality.

On the other hand social opinions and political actions still largely follow the old narrow-minded thinking. In global politics the small-state mentality still prevails, just as it characterised Germany in the late Middle Ages. Progress is only made very slowly and with difficulty. In this sense one can talk of territorial limitations.

A further important point is the division of human society into social classes, interest groups, political movements, groups with cultural, religious, philosophical orientations etc. In this respect, many boundaries and fissures run through the middle of human society. This aspect can be combined with the concept of cultural narrowness.

In relation to both forms of limitations the following two aspects should be noted:

- On the one hand, there is the identity-forming aspect. Thus, in the same way that every human being, because of his nature, has his own, quite unique perception, view of life and aesthetic, and in the same way that he is a unique being, so this also applies to groups. Every group has a unique cultural or also territorial identity and is characterised by special attributes, which are regarded by the members as similarities. From this perspective, the boundaries make the individual attributes of the respective regions, the respective countries, the cultural community etc. distinguishable and identifiable.
- Secondly, there is the aspect of contrariness. The characteristics of a spatially or culturally definable community in many cases contradict, or are even in conflict with, the characteristics and approaches of other communities.

While the identity-forming aspect ensures that human society features structures, diverse facets and cultural wealth, an area of conflict that is just as diverse results from the aspect of contrariness which makes the development of the mankind organism into an, in part, dramatically ongoing process.

Of course, there has to be this area of conflict today and also in the future. It is not possible to have the one without the other, namely where there are differences and identities there will always be tensions. Furthermore, as in the individual's neural mechanism, here the differential functional principle applies, namely the stimulus for further development results from disagreements and the incentive to resolve these.

However, the question is how to deal with the contradictions and the fact that these will always be there. In this respect it is particularly important to distinguish between the really human way of confronting these, and the way that is characterised by historical burdens.

In part, there has already been a really human way of dealing with conflicts for a long time. The ability to manage conflict and conflict resolution are something that one can learn and practice. The parameters are well known. Particularly important characteristics are mutual respect and dealing with one another in a more respectful way. What is essential is that one is willing to learn, about others and from others, that one is met with tolerance, that there is communication, that one is willing to compromise.

Another more important factor is also clearly the will and the opportunity to satisfy the demands of the pyramid of needs. It is important that both sides in the conflict are mutually entitled to the right to satisfy all needs. But it is also important that there are in fact positive developments in this respect. If there are none of these – and this is because of an objective shortage of resources - conflict resolution is doomed to failure.

In addition to the fact that the strategies and attitudes that are needed for conflict resolution are known in principle, and in this respect human beings increasingly possess useful know-how, unfortunately it must also be asserted that there are many examples of behaviour which are based on a criminal disregard for this know-how.

This has primarily something to do with historical burdens. It has something to do with the fact that there are still many niches in which locally developed strategies and ways of thinking appear to be sufficient. And it has something to do with the fact that human society as a whole is still far from having climbed the pyramid of needs, that there are still many regions, countries, regimes, social classes in which the fulfilment of needs does not really work, or within which this is perhaps not yet officially declared to be desirable, in terms of important categories of needs.

The important fundamental problems here are a restricted perception horizon resulting from historical roots, a lack of knowledge transfer, and inadequate resolution strategies and model concepts. In particular, the attitude of individual partners in conflict is regularly based on old disputes and claims instead of a wide-ranging look to the future.

However, the process of coalescence is in full swing. Common points of contact and interdependencies are becoming more and more numerous. The impending disasters are assuming an increasingly global nature. Mankind as a whole is being challenged more and more. It is condemned to shared decline or to shared success.

3.4 The trend towards subtlety

From history and the present one could conclude that there can never be a world without violence and war. This can be countered by the following:

- There will never be a world without conflicts.
- The way in which conflicts are carried out is always changing.

- In the optimistic case, the world could develop in such a way that physical force and wars become increasingly rare.

In fact, the upward trend in human society is linked to a trend in increasing subtlety in the emergence and unfolding of conflicts. What is consistently irritating here, unfortunately, is the fact that western democracies in which human rights are supposed to be upheld also consistently start wars. This is particularly related to the threat of an objective lack of resources (oil, raw materials etc.), which, however, accrues not least from the exaggerations of the market economy and the consumer society and the growing hunger for resources which constantly results from this. Basically, though, the trend towards subtlety cannot be denied.

In particular where it is possible, with a certain stability, for a relatively high percentage of the population to achieve a certain prosperity, and where democracy and human rights prevail as a valuable asset, conflicts are handled quite differently from regions where poverty, possibly still coupled with feudal/mafia-like/corrupt methods of leadership, predominates. In advanced countries there are no fewer problems and conflicts, which are fought over and debated endlessly, but this rarely leads to violent actions.

In these societies it also results in frustration, exclusion, relative poverty, repression, crime and many other negative actions. Life is no less marked by inconsistencies and disaster than in less advanced countries. However, all this takes place at a higher level of subtlety. The potential for conflict is basically no less. However, the trend is that conflict resolution increasingly only occurs "in the head", in interpersonal communication and in economic parameters, and less and less in terms of physical damage.

From the differential functional principle of the human brain, from the fact that the potential for activity basically derives from the motive of overcoming negative emotions, the result is that a pure principle of happiness cannot function. Thus as, objectively, a shortage of resources is constantly occurring and must be combated, the human being, in the mind and in interpersonal relations, also basically always needs a negative experience in order to strive for fulfilment.

This means that there cannot be a life without pressure and also that there are always winners and losers. However, a very widespread renunciation of physical force should, probably, be possible in principle.

In all the advances that have already been achieved in this respect in western democracies, it should not be forgotten that the material prosperity that prevails there has up to now, in many cases, been built on the extreme exploitation of poorer regions. Affluent societies export their shady side, such as for example their waste, to other regions of the world that are as far distant as possible. Children in poor countries have to be exploited and slowly poisoned for fashionable clothes, which are sold with high margins in rich countries. From this perspective, for a long time affluent countries have not presented a really good example.

3.5 *Mind, awfulness effect and belief*

As human society moves upwards, there is the problem that the mind often faces the need to withstand major tensions. Life happens in a comparatively barbaric reality, whereas one wants to do a good deed or make a progressive contribution. Both ethical motivations and outstanding intellectual, manual, artistic, sporting achievements etc. can only develop on the basis of pronounced imagination and sensitivity, as well as mental complexity. Subtle neural processes are needed for this, the subjects and results of which rise far above the immediate experience, or above the current facts of life. Here, however, there is the contradiction that, the higher the demands and goals, the higher the complexity level of the neural processes and the more subtly perception functions, bad experiences that are realised in the living environment are at the same time inevitably all the more intolerable. A mind that is particularly well prepared for the challenges of the future and is focused on the welfare of the community, that embodies a high degree of aesthetics and anticipates the demand for a high-grade fulfilment of the pyramid of needs, is also at the same time particularly exposed to an awfulness effect in the perception of current reality.

This conflict, which is present in every human being, leads to pressure to control the perception of reality. It will require something to explain the deep divide between demand and reality. It will require something constant, to which one can hold on to, something that gives comfort, that in the end, nevertheless, enables the reality to appear in a positive light. Finally one has the choice between a relatively realistic, pragmatic way of life, which, however, blocks the way to domains that require more complex, subtle, sensitive emotional experiences, or a way of life which adds explanations, assumptions, models or spiritual elements to this perception, which makes dealing with this emotional experience possible and tolerable, despite everything.

In a living environment which puts almost insurmountable obstacles in the way of a fulfilled life in terms of the pyramid of needs, explanatory models which can be shared with many fellow human beings are particularly helpful. It is almost inevitable that the human being is involved in cultural processes that offer both an explanation and also communality. As human beings are not rational creatures and scientific explanatory models were neither quickly available, nor generally accessible, nor incorporate an ethic, but instead tend to require this, this need must have led, and must lead, to the development of religions and ethical teachings.

The creation of communities on the basis of such systems can in particular fill in the following two gaps:

- Community explanatory models and ethical norms allow a tolerable interaction with living conditions. They offer consolation and hope. In this way it becomes possible for awareness to develop new domains and thus prepare the way for a progressive development. A particularly complex mind requires a particularly good foundation, in terms of the lower levels of the pyramid of needs. A situation that must lead to extreme frustrations, rationally speaking, is in this sense best compensated for by a form of community solidarity offering hope. From this perspective belief can move mountains, and without ethical norms and teachings, religions and progressive philosophies of life, there would only have been a clearly reduced opportunity for the trend towards subtlety.
- Communities offer a platform for the fulfilment of needs at levels 4B and 5B of the pyramid of needs. It is precisely in living environments shaped by

poverty and repression, crime and violence, in which it is partly a case of naked survival, that the conditions for the long-lasting fulfilment of individual needs, the need for recognition, self-fulfilment and mental growth, are particularly poor. A community that devotes itself to the cultivation of ethical, religious, spiritual systems can fill this gap particularly well in these particular conditions.

The formation of communities that are committed to ethical, religious, spiritual goals and philosophies of life, offering hope, are therefore an important basis for the fact that an upright gait, in the psychological sense, can develop at all. The fact that developments can result which lead to community solidarity of as many people as possible under the umbrella of doctrine, philosophy of life or religion, is, as far as possible, beneficial for progressive developments in human society. However, unfortunately configurations also regularly result in this context in which this positive effect is reversed.

Every philosophy of life is based on some assumptions and commitments which may be markedly progressive when they were established, and in relation to the situation in which the society in question finds itself. An important basis for success and the beneficial effect of a philosophy of life or religion is the community belief in a few important principles. A disposition towards a certain claim to absolute power, a claim to totalitarianism, a claim to universality and a suggestive effect thus achieved can be beneficial for the creation of a broad basis in the population. But even from this situation, particularly under the following conditions, the result can have serious potential for destructiveness:

- Later, if on the basis of a new stage of development

of society one of the principles turns out to be a shackle, it is all the more difficult to shake off.

- If borders between countries and communities shift, one of the principles can lead to conflict with other cultures, religions and philosophies of life. It can even be the case that a religion or doctrine is already created in such a conflict and this is its constant companion.

Both points result in the need to primarily follow such models and perceptions, which can be sufficient for the idea of a horizon defined as broadly as possible and with as much tolerance as possible for other opinions and religions. An especially positive example is the creed of "Bahai", which proclaims "a message of mutual tolerance, respect for all religions, social reform and international justice" (Stanford 2010, 173, Section 43: "Contemporary credos"). Essentially, however, all world religions and all important doctrines involve corresponding elements of tolerance towards those of different faiths. Unfortunately, however, there are constantly followers who would like to deny this.

3.6 The human being as a mandate holder

The human mind strives to make his own life good enough. That one's own needs are of paramount importance compared with fellow humans has nothing to do with egotism; rather it is necessarily caused by the fact that each kind of stimulus available is primarily based on one's own needs. But if the individual is able to recognise himself to be a member of society, and in particular to construct the higher needs to accommodate this fact, then this will consistently result in behaviour which is beneficial for fellow humans and society. Though the opportunity to avoid egotistical attitudes is only possible if simultaneously a certain level of healthy fulfilment of one's own needs is achieved.

Every individual, as a social being, is dependent on companionship and, vice versa, he influences the development of a group, a community and the mankind organism as a whole. Simply the fact that one exists, breathes, consumes food, exchanges goods and words, is enough to exert influence. Also death does not immediately eliminate influence; rather it causes an additional stimulus. The situation is particularly good if democracy is practised in a way which provides citizens with the ability to be involved in political processes. But even without these pre-conditions no-one is without influence, and, besides politics, a democratically organised society also has many other areas in which it can be created.

Thus the individual is well advised to understand himself to be an influencing factor. **Each human being is equipped with a natural mandate to determine how global human society is arranged and developed.** This is an inevitable fact, which one can either accept or refuse. The latter attitude might be based on the assumption that influence can be avoided, but it is really no more than a vote for conservatism or fatalism. To use more positive words: the political passivity of some citizens has the role of supporting social stability, which nevertheless must be indicated as an impact.

The natural mandate means, again, that every citizen, as part of his socialisation, as well as all other burdens, is scarcely able to get away from his role as a politician and philosopher. It is assumed that this is a principle which may not be met sufficiently, but which cannot in general be avoided.

3.7 *The social power system*

The assumption of a natural mandate in the configuration of the global cultural society contradicts the picture of the human being of the present, who is perhaps a skilled worker or an expert in one or several areas, and who also cultivates a few hobbies, if he actually has the opportunity. Moreover, there are experts who concern themselves with bigger issues like macroeconomics, philosophy, politics, industry etc. In more or less broad parameters, everyone is concerned with his current area of expertise, his current occupation, making a living, as well as – as far as possible – friendships, family, sport, fun, games and recreation. Where possible he also becomes involved in social welfare or strives for self-fulfilment in one direction or another. Why should one want to read more into the system of social relations?

Quite simple: because the democratically-humanistically organised society and the ability of the global population to master their fate stands or falls with this!

A group consists of all its members, human society consists of all human beings. Each person participates in developing the community and influences it – even if he is not aware of this or if he is inclined to deny this fact.

Two aspects should be noted here: on the one hand it concerns the creative influence that every member of society exerts, on the other hand it is about political influence. Both are closely related. Based on the assumption that creative activities also always have a certain indirect political effect, the political dimension of social interactions should particularly be considered here.

Of course, it is the case that not every citizen exerts influence on social processes to the same degree, it is in fact clear that the effects which different people exert can differ greatly from each other in terms of their intensity. But, as stated, no-one has no influence. The vector diagram in figure 3 helps to make it clear how social power (SP) can be assembled from many individual powers (IP1–4). The projection IP1 – IP2' – IP3' – IP4' gives the direction and value of the power arrow of social power SP.

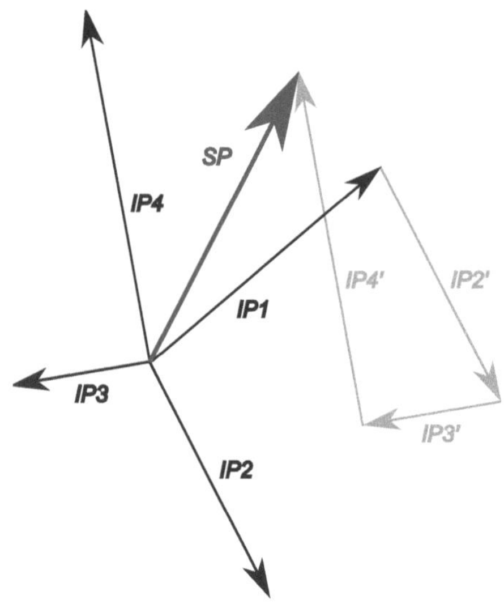

Figure 3 – Social power system

Society can be considered as a polydimensional system of power, in which every subsystem controls the development of a particular aspect. It is certainly not the case that every citizen influences all aspects of life, but each one influences some of the aspects, and there are again countless interactions between the aspects. That life is endlessly complicated – and that this trend is increasing – is in any case clear. However, it is definitely sensible here to consider specific aspects separately. As already suggested above, in this respect there is a question which should be regarded as particularly important, namely that of how well democracy works and which aspects should be considered when answering this question.

A democracy works so much better if the equilibrium between the influences which all citizens exert on political decisions is more balanced. From this viewpoint, the ideal situation would be reached if all citizens were involved in every decision with a power arrow of exactly the same size. With a referendum this ideal is almost achieved – everyone has just one vote.

In real life, such an ideal situation is at best temporary and only achievable for a few political decisions. The level of the achievable balance of citizen participation in political decisions is on the whole normally considerably lower. However, it can be noted that democracy is a state of affairs in which influence on politics is distributed with a certain level of balance to all citizens.

The following are particular reasons for a clear deviation from the ideal situation:

- Not every citizen can and wants to be an expert on every area. Not every citizen can concern himself with all aspects of politics. Not everyone believes that all individual political decisions are important or interesting. For this reason, there is the possibility of temporarily transferring part of one's own right to exert an influence by proxy to people or to parties. An important basis for this is confidence that the most significant interests are protected here in the right way.

- Life is not only about the legislative, executive and plebiscites, but is influenced by many further social forces, laws and constraints. In this it is normal that individual actors are given the opportunity to exert disproportionate influence.

Metaphorically speaking, every human being therefore has a power arrow or a lever to influence political events, but this power arrow differs in strength, or the length of the lever can vary greatly. Most people will be inclined to define their own lever as being extremely short, or as largely or completely ineffective. This is related to the large number of fellow human beings with whom one usually shares a place in life. But precisely with the example of a plebiscite it can easily be observed that the decision is based on nothing other than the sum of all votes cast. In this case there is no other influence, provided that it is all executed accurately. At least here it is clear that it depends on every vote.

In other cases, such as that of representative democracy, it is already less clear. Here the impression can be given that trust is regularly given to the wrong politicians, that the right alternatives are not available and that how political decisions are actually made is hardly transparent.

Even worse are the circumstances in political systems with dogmatic, dictatorial or corrupt elements and in regimes that are hostile to human rights. Here there is the particular case that the possibility of political influence by normal citizens has little importance, or is undermined or even completely negated. In addition there is frequently a danger to livelihoods or life and limb if the compliance needed is missed.

However, here as well, every citizen has an effect on the political system which is not equal to zero. The following figures show an example of a model dictatorship with a dictator (DP1), a government official (GP1) and 20 citizens (CP1–20).

The resulting social power is again represented by the blue arrow (SP). The 20 citizens stand, for example, for 20 million citizens with very short power arrows. With the government official, it is assumed that he stands for ten thousand somewhat more influential people. For the sake of simplicity the dictator in the model wants to go left, and all the citizens want something else, but are not agreed on the direction.

Figure 4 shows a situation in which the citizens as a whole are largely politically indifferent, so that the dictator can autocratically define the rules.

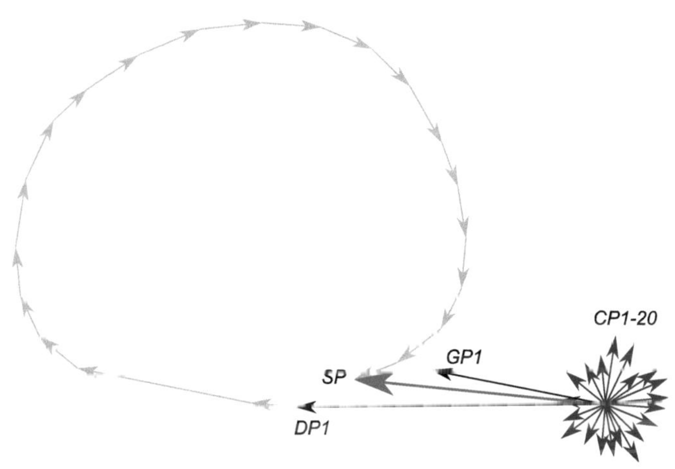

Figure 4 – Dictator and citizens 1

Figure 5 shows a situation in which powers already form in a certain direction. This could be caused by the aggravation of grievances and reprisals. But it is still not enough to depose the dictator. However, his room for manoeuvre has already become much smaller.

In figure 6 finally the situation has arisen which every dictator must fear – unsustainable situations have united the citizens and also some of the more influential people to the extent that the downfall of the dictator is no longer to be prevented. The slow transformation of the balance of power has led to the political balance being overturned.

Why this digression? What does it achieve to describe these apparently rather banal principles? Quite recently, with Tunisia, the Arab Spring gave us the best example that a popular uprising can work. With further developments, in particular also in Egypt, we also see that life is complicated and that there are never any simple solutions and clear successes.

It is established that the perception, behaviour and actions of every individual count. Irrespective of whether the individual wants to accept that or not – he always has influence in the social power system, which eventually also has a noticeable effect.

If one accepts this fact, the result is that in every case it is more clever to always make the trade-off between the demand to shape one's personal life – which already incorporates higher levels of need and altruistic modes of behaviour – and the demand to also think about the fate of society and the whole of mankind. The distinctive ability to at least temporarily renounce individual sensitivities in order to jointly force through an important demand should here be the essential key to solving polit-

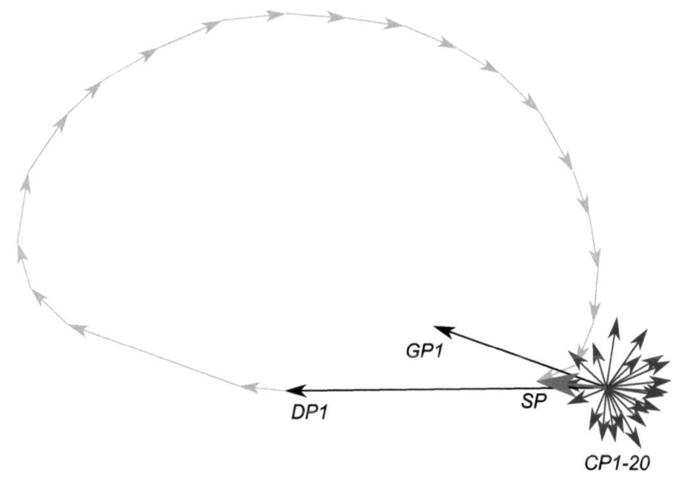

Figure 5 – Dictator and citizens 2

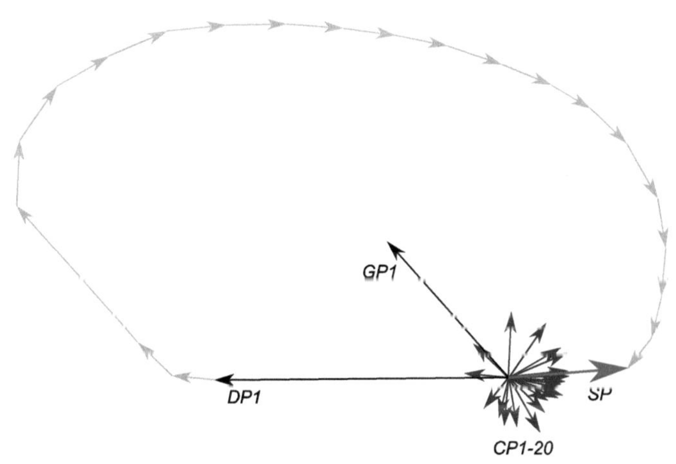

Figure 6 – Dictator and citizens 3

ical problems. If this ability remains underdeveloped, conflicts and crises that get out of hand are inevitable.

The mankind organism only has a chance, then, if most of its members play a useful part in its further development. There is no other authority and no mechanism which could direct the development of this organism in a suitable direction in an amazing way. It can therefore not be at all harmful to also raise the perception in this regard, and to act accordingly.

Every human being is constantly concerned with the trade-off between one's own well-being and the common good. With the common good, however, the question has to be answered of how far it extends and how large the family to which one feels that one belongs is defined. If one were to consider the trend towards the coalescence of mankind, the answer could therefore be that all humans are included.

In the end, the chances that politics can manage the common good successfully depends on the trend of the respective trade-offs by all citizens. The narrower citizens define their family circle, the poorer are the chances for the common good and the greater the contradiction between the sense of entitlement towards politics and the opportunities for politics to satisfy this. Ultimately the sum of the relevant trade-offs of all citizens determines how good are the chances for the common good.

3.8 Precision and blockades of perception

There are different findings and opinions on the question of the accuracy and precision which the human perception mechanism is capable of. Apart from a few systematic misperceptions, which are related to the functioning of the relevant organs and projection fields of the cortex, it can, however, be assumed that perception is possible with extremely high levels of precision. This is mainly restricted by the limits of resolution of the sensory organs. However, what is possible within the framework of these limits can also be used, in principle.

Performances which are regularly achieved in sporting competitions support this assumption. Here it also appears that this statement is not only true for the faculty of perception, but also for the sensorimotor part of the human control mechanism. Top athletes consistently amaze with new outstanding achievements but this just shows what potential there is in all of us.

So much for the practicability of signal processing with active humans or mammals. What about, though, the intellectual, cognitive, artistic abilities, processing the complex content of the senses and the ability to judge situations accurately and exhaustively, as well as making sensible decisions? How accurately can the recombination products produced in the simulation mode of the brain represent the environment and how precisely is it possible to plan and to make changes?

There has long been evidence that in this respect humans are in principle capable of extreme, outstanding achievements. The scientific-technical revolution alone is evidence enough. It is true that we cannot draw the conclusion from this development that humans are in general guiding lights, but at least a few examples of humankind must occasionally have had enlightened moments, however, otherwise the rapid progress of the most recent centuries would not have been possible.

However, experiences from history and everyday life also show that man's path through countless trials and tribulations is marked out, indeed that behaviour often, apparently, even causes goal-oriented destruction and self-destruction. Accidents, collapsing buildings, aggressive disputes, wars, threats to the environment, divorces, business failures etc. are not generally traced back to the primary intentions of those people who have, however, helped to make such things happen. Why is there this contradiction? Why is man capable of extreme achievements and then also of more or less major blunders and misjudgements?

There could be many answers to this but we should mention two aspects here. The most important aspect is certainly the fact that humans are constantly confronted with objective difficulties. In order to cope with a situation, first technical skills and knowledge must be acquired. The way to do this is experience. This could also be expressed thus: If something goes wrong, the actors involved were probably "beginners" and if they have survived the experience, then there is the chance to slowly become a "Pro". The path to awareness consists of trial and error.

However, as well as this there is a second important aspect which results from the Maslowian principle of the relative prepotency of needs. First of all this principle says that human activity is always aimed at a need or needs which indicate the greatest deficiency. The result of this is also that higher needs and intellectual and artistic achievements can only then gain in importance if lower needs are successfully satisfied. This initially expresses the fact that coping with everyday life is the requirement for being able to aspire to greater things.

If one leaves these boundary conditions to one side and concentrates only on the achievements of the neural system, with the simplified assumption that all lower needs are fulfilled, this in no way means, however, that the prepotency of boundary conditions no longer plays any role. The brain can also then not really escape the principle that all neural processes are sensitive to context and are accompanied by emotions if there are no objective reasons for this.

It is much more related to the brain's functional principle, that all processes are basically accompanied by a certain delusion. Every aspiration, also at the highest intellectual level, is accompanied by motivations, which have their roots in the relationship of actors to their natural and social environment.

Here as well, two aspects must be considered. On the one hand, there should be a basis for relationships and material requirements for the particular activity. Artists need the public and a minimum amount of food. Craftspeople need orders. Engineers and architects rely on this to obtain a project. Workers need a job. For a cosy get-together, one needs friends and good acquaintances. Scientists need platforms for exchanging scientific experience and a budget. For a culture of protest one needs like-minded people. Those involved in charity rely on the cooperation of those in need of support and require an aid agency for whom they can work.

On the other hand, there needs to be a subject which the ambition can focus on. The basis of relationships for being active can possibly be created, particularly if it concerns actors who deal with the purpose of self-fulfilment. A firm or organisation that may be needed can be established, a budget can be applied for or procured, a job can be looked for, a public can be gained. However, what is left if everything goes well at this level is in fact the need for ambition to be focused on a subject. This results ultimately in possibilities for what can be achieved. At the same time, though, this also always means that a certain focus is established and themes that are located outside a certain horizon must be faded out. This also concerns the question of the limited resources which the individual possesses to lead his life, his need for know-how and his projects. Thus in the best case the result is always perceptions, awareness, attitudes, achievements and actions which are determined by focusing on the particular context.

This works wonderfully, as long as this is the right priority. With rapid developments in the present age it is clear, however, that any domains quickly change, that borders are shifted with great rapidity, that narrow-minded thinking is increasingly dubious. Jobs and hobbies alter their character or disappear, new ones emerge. Interdisciplinary modes of operation are increasingly necessary. Country borders are playing an increasingly minor role. The knowledge of human beings is growing phenomenally and conventions quickly change or intermingle.

Therefore there is always a conflict between a relatively clear perception of a few, more or less narrowly delimited subjects and an obscured perception of many other aspects of life. It is clear here that the most important area of work, on which one must be an expert, is always how to organise one's own life. A lot depends on this, how the family and professional development and social relationships are successfully channelled in directions which appear to be acceptable. Only in this respect does the possibility and at the same time the need develop to be successfully active in other areas. With the high level of dynamism with which life changes, there are increasingly frequent clashes with requirements for which one is not prepared and which have to be tackled by constant struggles for new skills and approaches.

As a result, we can propose the hypothesis that impaired perception and deficient actions are rather the norm than the exception. Here again are a few reasons for this as a summary:

- Lower needs temporarily have priority.
- Earlier severe frustrations or traumatic experiences exert an influence. This can continue over several generations.
- Boundary conditions resulting from family, professional and other social environments assert their influence.
- Skills and competence profiles acquired up to now shape the perception and lead to an unbalanced assessment of the circumstances.
- Position in society obstructs views of other destinies, classes or castes.
- Professional integration influences ways of thinking and acting.
- Geographical or national aspects shape perceptions.
- Current or past projects represent aspects with a strong influence on attitudes and aims.
- With ownership comes responsibility.
- Everything is also a question of belief and trust.
- Finally it comes down to the question of what one has shares in, or where one is thinking of investing in the future, by whatever means. Perception and behaviour must also comply with this. Only dropouts can free themselves from this constraint, but they do not determine which path the world takes

and besides, dropping out is if anything a special attitude, with limited possibilities for realisation.

Here we should in no way put the case for the Marxist materialistic assumption “Being determines consciousness”. It is not about denying the perceptibility and suggestibility of the world through the self-conscious mind of the individual. In contrast the assessment mechanism enables man to control his life and to influence his environment.

But the point is that there is a range of apparent explanations that the results of perception are often remarkably or positively wrong. The outcome of this is also that this inclination towards fallibility and a lack of precision is indeed an inherently principled phenomenon which, on the other hand, however, is not general, but only contextually effective. Therefore in principle there must also be boundary conditions under which the neural mechanism works in a very precise and efficient way and under which it almost reflects reality truthfully. When it matters, humans even know how to find the means and the method to transcend the boundaries of their five senses and to extend the perception and actions with success to entities which were originally not imaginable. Here as well the principle of trial and error applies and here as well the interpretation of the results is in principle normally first subject to all kinds of errors. But here as well, the potential for awareness is related to this – the scientific-technical revolution proves it.

What is the purpose, then, of these discussions? The point is to reinforce the following conclusions:

- Imprecise results of perception and errors are a normal, inherently principled occurrence in the neural mechanism, which results in particular from its contextual mode of operation.

- Precisely because of the dependence of neural achievements on the context, in principle there are also no boundaries of accuracy and cognitive faculty which cannot be exceeded, if the context is suitably justified.

Finally the perception horizon determines the cognitive faculty that can be attained. The conditionality of life, from which one can never really completely free oneself, always restricts horizons one way or another. Liberation from this stranglehold is achievable, however, partially and temporarily. It is worth striving to use the AA, not only for a crude assessment and to control attention to the alternatives, which are imposed on the respective context, but above all also for the active development of alternative perception horizons. Human beings' prospects of being able to accurately understand and beneficially influence their own life and the social and natural environment thereby increase.

A crucial factor is also the context of accountability in which the actor moves. In the context of a beer table discussion or an anonymous internet blog it is easy to advance major arguments, as well as to prove independence and a broad horizon. At the same time it is also relatively worthless, except for the actor's salvation, which is also of course eminently important, or as a preliminary exercise for genuine actions.

It is something quite different to have to also vouch for what one discloses, to have to publicly put one's head and one's own name on the line. In the latter case it is in principle not possible to ignore any boundary conditions. From this perspective it is no wonder that human society finds it difficult to maintain a course which is beneficial for the common good, while there is no shortage of banal ideas for solutions.

3.9 The professionalism trend and its side effects

In relation to the scientific-technical revolution, the conflict between the necessary focus on particular issues of thought and actions and the need to observe the social environment normally is raised to a new level. The know-how available to humanity is evolving at an explosive rate. A particular role is also played here by the growing ability to divide up the organisation of work and social life with increasing efficiency. An individual member can concern himself with growing intensity with an increasingly small fragment of social activities. By means of this constantly advancing process, society succeeds in developing extreme potential and continuing to advance the scientific-technical revolution. So, through the increase in research, development and professional specialisation, innovative discoveries are made again and again, solutions to increase productivity are found and past errors are revealed.

But at the same time problems, risks and temptations also result from this development, which can affect the development of society. So the trend towards professionalism has the following side effects, amongst others:

- The individual human being is concerned with increasing intensity with a more and more restricted variety of issues. As well as the possibility of being so much more efficient in the relevant area of expertise, at the same time, though, this means a thorough narrowing of the horizon.

- The effort of acquiring new knowledge and developing new technologies is constantly increasing. Where previously individuals could still achieve ground-breaking progress at relatively amateurish levels, today large, if possible internationally active teams cooperate in order to achieve comparably relative progress at today's level.
- This progress only still seems to be possible in areas which before would have been chosen as important by a significant or powerful part of society. The requirement is always that it should seem worthwhile to make an investment in any form. This can be a monetary investment – with money from the state, from the private sector, from an organisation, from a foundation etc. However, this can also be a cultural investment, in which humans take part in combined activities in their commitment to art, environment, religion, welfare, sport etc.
- In relation to professionalisation and the increasing demands for scientific work, there is an increase in barriers to creative interdisciplinary contributions, which if possible could be provided by individuals or small groups. On the one hand this is logical, on the other hand, however, it is also questionable. In principle this leads to a dramatic reduction in the probability that unpredictable perceptions are brought to light in interdisciplinary areas, because it is not possible to spend the appropriate effort that would be needed for this. It promotes the likelihood that humanity moves in a cycle of blindness, in which influential groups suggest all aims reciprocally, but where the opportunity for intelligent cooperation in all segments, and emergence and innovation at the level of society as a whole, is minimised.

- This questionable development also expresses itself, amongst other things, in the use of language. In many areas it is common to use language as a bulwark against undesirable invaders, by quite deliberately using a terminology which is separate from the common use of language. Of course it is inevitable that language that is specific to a domain should contain complex terminologies which are only developed on the basis of specialist training. The professionalisation of social processes is, however, often related to the fact that broad cooperation on linguistic fields is avoided as far as possible.
- The trend towards professionalisation has therefore become a professionalism barrier which continues to mount up the more human knowledge grows. This barrier in particular appears to hinder the possibility of the development of human society being evaluated and organised just as professionally as happens in individual, mostly small, subdomains.
- At the same time, at any moment there are also powers which counteract this trend. So the market for popular science literature is booming in educationally advanced countries. New trends, crucial incentives for new discoveries and outstanding achievements often come from environments that do not seem a priori to be created for this. Subcultures and protest cultures, as well as civil society, regularly influence this development to a large extent. However, the development that results from these two opposing trends depends critically on which priorities society sets in relation to its value system, and to what degree it allows plurality.

Finally, the conclusion is obvious that the scientific-technical revolution has indeed produced remarkable results, which could act as a wonderful foundation for the prosperity of the whole of humanity, but that at the same time the result is a trend towards the narrowing of the perception horizon and to blind spots on the horizon of understanding, which can have fatal consequences. This explains why the development of expert knowledge on the global system of human society and the ability to adequately develop this system cannot keep pace with rapid technical and economic developments.

It should be mentioned that professionalism also in part usually consists of concealing substantial deficits or distinct interests and hiding behind a, to some degree, beautiful, professional and enticing-looking facade.

3.10 Aesthetics and society

In the chapter "The neural system" it was established that the functioning of the human neural system follows the Aesthetics Principle and that the Aesthetics Principle rules the world.

What are the consequences for human society?

It does not follow from the Aesthetics Principle that the world must primarily be characterised by aestheticism, that all human beings should become "true aesthetes", that life should above all comprise so-called beautiful things. Of course, art, culture and etiquette are important aspects which play a particular, hopefully growing, role as motivation. That is also an important part, but not the essence of the Aesthetics Principle.

Following the Aesthetics Principle in fact means noticing the fact that the emotional sphere generally takes priority over the material sphere.

This means:

- That the satisfaction of needs is achieved by nothing other than feelings.
- That the areas of conflict and objectives to which human ambition is directed primarily exist in the world of feelings and only indirectly, conveyed by the world of feelings, in the real world.
- That contradictions between negative and positive feelings are the engine of any human activity. The worse the frustrations and the more wonderful the hopes, then an even stronger stimulus is possible.
- That ultimately with all living conditions, processes, actions and results, the feelings and perceptions which this provokes in humans are what counts first and foremost.
- That a priori the human being seeks nothing other than all possible forms of aesthetics, i. e. living conditions and experiences that convey good feelings.
- That in the pyramid of needs the aesthetic side generally carries more weight than the material side.
- That the feeling that material factors are of the utmost importance not only results from the fact that they are an important requirement for the satisfaction of needs – that alone would not suffice –, but also that worlds of feelings arise via the projection spaces of the body and the environment and develop their dynamic. However, this does not mean that material factors take priority or that there is a com-

parable or primary position. Because a material living condition, once it is defined as desirable, must not inevitably also lead to the fulfilment of a need when it occurs, but a positive feeling is already fulfilment.

But what does that mean now for life in the present, for the existence of the individual, and for the development of society and the whole of humanity? This question will be examined in the following chapters.

3.11 The cultural currency system

Is there an aesthetic currency?

Yes, one could see it in such a way. Any interactions with the environment and one's own body, as well as every kind of communication, is linked to the pursuit of aesthetic fulfilment, which includes the fulfilment of basic needs. If one applies the concept of currency to a universal means of exchange within human society, the result is therefore that with every kind of communication and interpersonal interaction an exchange takes place implicitly in the aesthetics currency. This principle is all-embracing. It is true, irrespective of whether the interaction proceeds directly or indirectly; thus the exchange is also included between humans who are living a long way from one another in time or in space. Amongst other things, all legends, written records and traditions of human history, all art works, as well as any knowledge and any education, represent a value in the aesthetics currency. This is true even more for all informal and physical items that are exchanged between human beings living in the present. The currencies and the amount of material products can be seen as a subset of the currency of aesthetics.

In contrast to the single currency, which represents money, the aesthetics currency is infinitely polymorphous. This inevitably results from the emergent nature of the neural system.

It could be asserted that culture is the currency of aesthetics – with reference to the following boundary conditions:

- Every human being has his own quite individual concept of culture, which as a rule overlaps with the cultural concept of fellow human beings, however.
- Culture is a social phenomenon and so it does not appear in humans per se, but always only in the interface between several people. The individual nature of the concept of culture in each human being is therefore always linked to relations with fellow human beings.

Important forms of the cultural currency are, for example, knowledge, know-how, all forms of expression of empathy and altruism, all forms of art, any achievements and potential for the organisation and structuring of social life, group life, family life, any forms of communication, any achievements and potential for satisfying needs on the social scale, including the needs of the material-economic sphere.

Answering the question of which coin is used for "payment" or which can be used for payment, is pointless. It would lead nowhere if one tried to assess and measure the cultural currency according to the standards of a monetary-material currency. This is not feasible because the system of cultural currencies is characterised by emergence, creativity, partial individuality and limited convertibility. Every cultural value is itself potentially confronted by any alternative cultural values. There can be similarities between cultural values, but also contradictions, antagonistic contradictions, areas of conflict. Only each individual human being can decide for himself to what extent whichever cultural value or other represents a concrete value.

With knowledge currency it is, for example, clear that in principle this is of eminent importance for every person. To what extent, however, a concrete knowledge component is really important, useful, realisable for a person, depends very strongly on educational background and the context of socialisation.

A particularly important question is the convertibility of the currency systems. From the creative nature of culture and the individual nature of perception and participation, the result is that the aesthetics currency or cultural currency, or however one wants to call it, consists of an infinite amount of partial currencies with limited convertibility. There are in fact partial currencies with a relatively high degree of convertibility, but in principle this always has a limit.

This is also true for monetary-material currencies. There are, it is true, a few monetary reserve currencies that are largely globally convertible and with which one can purchase material goods everywhere. However, this is only true of the material-monetary aspect of the pyramid of needs. Society is in fact characterised by the intensive exchange between the cultural-aesthetic sphere and the material-monetary sphere, but in this system money and material ownership are only partly convertible. It is not possible "to buy" any forms of culture. Particularly important in this regard is the conclusion that primacy lies in the cultural-aesthetic side of the currency systems, which again inevitably results from the primarily aesthetic-emotional fulfilment principle of human needs.

The apparently particularly high convertibility of monetary currencies can lead to the assumption that money rules the world. However, with an increasing level of education and a growing distance from emergency needs, it is clear that there are many assets that displace money and that also first restore money to its value. Finally know-how takes a key position in any successful economic activity and the most important key to know-how is human creativity. Again, this is not only motivated by the demand to earn money, but rather by the desire to be able to lead a life characterised by aesthetics and culture.

The assumption that cultural exchange and cultural values have a greater importance than economic aspects does not represent a danger for the commercial-economic side of life. Quite the contrary, strongholds of education policy and culture are usually sources of economic prosperity, and cultural and aesthetic requirements are an excellent basis for a good increase in demand.

That cultural values and feelings are more important than material values does not mean that it would be unnecessary or scandalous to accept payment or fees for accomplishments. Monetary remuneration is instead a need, as the human being must usually use at least part of his power to provide for the satisfaction of material needs and to cover monetary costs which accumulate as part of his activity. Furthermore, as a general rule payment also represents gratification, an acknowledgement of the work performed. Therefore it also has an intangible component. This is a sign of the close relationship which exists between the two spheres.

3.12 *The Culture Principle*

The stimulus of the neural system in an individual results from the Aesthetics Principle. The constant conflict with the conditions affecting aesthetic perceptions and the continued search for opportunities for improvement is what drives and motivates human beings. Here basic needs are only part of the full spectrum of projection fields. Another part of the spectrum concerns material conditions, where again there is an overlap with basic needs. However, on the whole the Aesthetics Principle involves much more than these two partial spectra. It also includes in particular higher levels of the aesthetic aspect of the pyramid of needs.

Translated to the community it follows that the stimulus for the development of social life is based on the Culture Principle, since culture is nothing other than the realisation of aesthetic demands in society. If one follows this principle, then the all-determining factor can only be the continued debate about the lack of cultural conditions in the social life. Of course here the question of opportunities for the fulfilment of basic needs, as well as the question of the distribution of material wealth, must also play a special role. Overall, however, it is about much more than this. It is about the organisation of cultural life as a whole. What is important about this is that the debate about the development of the social life is not controlled by the debate on material distribution, and that the principle of the maximisation of material gain and monetary-economic productivity is not made absolute. Instead reality is only taken into account if it is acknowledged that it is about a variety of cultural values, also in particular about values which cannot be obtained for all the money in the world.

In the ecological debate, the idea of tackling environmental damage is discussed, damage which is caused by the use of resources that is characterised by profit-seeking, by quantifying its material value and thus factoring this damage into the equation. This idea is a step in the right direction, but the perception is too narrow. This is because it follows the inclination to the absolute supremacy of the material-monetary principle.

In contrast, following the Culture Principle means establishing the likely fact that there are cultural-aesthetic values which are not achievable by material-monetary values, that the cultural-aesthetic sphere naturally has the dominant role, and that the material-monetary sphere only acquires its importance within cultural-aesthetic developments.

There are far-reaching consequences from this.

These are, in particular, that in principle it is not acceptable to cause damage to culture and to the environment in the name of increasing productivity or in the name of maximising profit without asking about the possibility of compensation for this. As stated above, the cultural-aesthetic currency probably consists of an infinite variety of partly convertible part currencies, where monetary-material part currencies are integrated into this system, but also with partial convertibility. In principle this means that a cultural asset can only then be damaged to create a material-monetary value if all human beings for whom this asset has a value agree with the compensation on offer. Depending on the progress made in the negotiations, this compensation could be of a material nature or it could be paid in some other kind of cultural-aesthetic currency. Mortgages can also only be included on this basis.

In relation to ecology and environmental protection, two aspects should be considered. On the one hand, the demand to conserve the environment is a cultural asset. Thus with regard to the question of whether environmental damage can be caused, the principle described above is just as valid as for any other cultural asset. Secondly, there is still in principle the hypothetical perception of all non-human creatures that are involved. As, however, it is very difficult to incorporate this, it implies allowing this factor, at least as defined by an additional commitment which respects fauna and flora, to have a particular intrinsic value.

Furthermore, it follows from the Culture Principle that the manner in which the globalising economic system treats the environment, human rights, poverty and conflicts today, with certain fatal tendencies, is an extreme aberration. There may overall be many different reasons for this. In relation to the value orientation of the western market economy, however, the inclination towards the absolute supremacy of the material-monetary principle, pronounced consumption and ignorance of cultural-aesthetic values is seen as an important reason for this aberration.

How can we find our way out of this dilemma, however? Against the demand to want to assert the Culture Principle we can say that society is directed towards the market economy by natural principles and stimuli. Human beings have chosen this form of society because it has apparently emerged through evolution as the best solution. The attempt to want to form a cultural society using warnings, or with dirigiste or even dictatorial means, follows neither the evolutionary approach, nor can it be described as being desired by human beings.

Can the Culture Principle nevertheless work in society? Which mechanisms and evolutionary approaches could there be?

First, the Culture Principle already works as a law of nature. It has been present in human society since there has been culture and higher needs. In western society, it is only eclipsed by the excessive belief in money and wealth. In history there are many cultures in which the Culture Principle had more prestige than is the case today in the western world and in the world that pursues globalisation.

Secondly, the Culture Principle asserts itself via the social discourse and the living culture. If social conventions are characterised by fixing on certain core values, it is always sensible to reflect on these core values and to ask the question of whether these should be justified. This debate could, then, lead to alternative views on the correct regulation of the market economy and social life as a whole. So the fact that a debate on the relationship between culture and market economy is ongoing in society can influence core values and give a new direction to the development of society.

Thirdly, there can be no question of a broad social consensus that the currently practised type of capitalist-market economy social order, including trends towards neoliberalism, globalisation, environmental destruction, ignorance of extreme global social differences and waging war for scarce resources, is the right way. Instead, the pent-up contradictions almost call for an outlet, for a reorientation of values and for significant modifications to the rules which apply to social life.

Fourthly, this is about the dialectic of social development. There have been many advanced civilisations which at one time became antiquated, however, and which were superseded by emerging forces and new variants of social agreement. So the progression of social orders is seen as a constant learning process that also, at the same time, increasingly takes the form of a process that takes place at global level. Here the capitalist-market economy phase may, if possible, answer the question of how sufficient productivity can be achieved. What can follow from this is a phase in which the relevant perceptions are not forgotten, but are put into perspective. That is comparable to growing up, in which a young organism accumulates unimagined powers and potential which it must, however, first learn to handle. Now it is a question of integrating the beloved new toys in a context in which they do not lead to certain self-destruction. It is a question of whether the self-conscious mind gains victory over the newly won instincts in every individual citizen, as well as globally.

From this perspective, capitalism is viewed as an important preparatory exercise for the global cultural society, which again cannot be dismissed as a utopia. At the same time, however, it is certain that the way to get there successfully should lead via a discourse with a high degree of complexity, and the result should then be characterised by a variety of cultural values, unimaginable until now.

3.13 The cultural-aesthetic perspective

It is essential that the development of humans and human society is determined primarily by the Aesthetics Principle that prevails for the neural system, and by the Culture Principle that prevails for social processes. The processes that are based on the exchange of monetary and material values are again almost equally important, and they have a close interrelationship with cultural-aesthetic processes; however, in a direct comparison they are in principle of secondary importance.

Based on the assumption that this thesis is correct, the arguments mentioned are valid, and that this view and an essential part of the secondary theses permanently withstand all examinations – then the question is asked of which conclusions are to be inferred from this for social life? The question is posed in particular in relation to the disastrous features of social development described in the first chapter.

The answer is: This thesis could provide a perspective which breaks away from the usual thought patterns and scientific domains, and it could therefore become an important starting point for a creative analysis of social processes and for new approaches.

A few widely-known thought patterns and polarities are those between “Right”, “Centre” and “Left” in the political spectrum, more or less market economy, more or less (neo-) liberalism, less or more regulation, autocracy and democracy, militarism and pacifism, market economy and planned economy, merit principle and equalisation, poverty and wealth. The statement that cultural and informational goods have a greater importance in society than money, indeed that they are closer to the primary motivation of human beings and that they are a more important basis for successful economic activity than financial resources, is basically a banal statement. At the same time, though, it can act as a source for many new perspectives on society, its problems and demands, as well as for new approaches.

Colin Crouch has referred to civil society and the need to secure progressive developments in small steps. The following answer was given on this above (see the section "Neoliberalism and contemporary capitalism"):

> "It would be better if one could also oppose the system of the global market, and of big business which systematically profits from it, using leverage in the form of a system, a paradigm, a common strategy."

The last few chapters tried to extract a new approach by comparing the material-monetary and the cultural-aesthetic spheres of society. And there is now an appropriate paradigm – in the form of an assertion that the Aesthetics Principle and the Culture Principle legally take priority over the prevailing complementary principle.

In particular, we can also draw the conclusion from this that the cautious attitude with which aesthetic and ethical standards typically oppose economic reason, or by which they can even be absorbed, are completely inadequate. It must be assumed that instead, inherent in these standards, there is an imperative nature, contempt for which carries a significant potential for risk. The fairy tale of the market as a natural law must therefore be opposed by the thesis that the cultural-aesthetic sphere of society contains a few categories, aspects, principles, rules and requirements, observance of which is at least just as advisable as is the case for economic laws. Perhaps it could be useful for the solution of some contemporary problems if they could also be analysed and assessed from this perspective.

If we wanted to try to follow this approach, this could then take place as part of the normal learning process that constantly occurs in all social spheres. Changes in paradigms that are due often happen here in an unspectacular way. However, with some of the current deficiencies, it is doubtful whether there is an adequate solution in this path that, to a certain extent, appears to be natural. In these cases it is if anything inevitable to identify in particular the disastrous dimension of events and to begin the struggle for unusual measures.

In the following chapters, a few attempts will be made to offer ideas and conclusions, observance of which may prove to be necessary with this in mind. In order to emphasise the imperative nature of the cultural-aesthetic perspective, in many cases real requirements are named, the fulfilment of which must be expressly sought in order to reach a solution. However, these demands should on no account be understood as dogma but as suggestions for objectives, which should be given a high priority. Which path will in fact finally be taken depends on the democratic political process and the creative actions of all citizens.

4 Culture and market economy

4.1 The contribution made by the market economy to culture

As stated above, the market economy is essentially based on the following two basic mechanisms:

- The law of supply and demand, also called the “invisible hand”.
- The principle of the increase in shareholder value.

History has shown that it is these mechanisms that in principle can make a useful contribution to the development of society. Countless attempts to organise life in the community in such a way that it is characterised by the stable fulfilment of needs, fairness, humanity, culture and peaceful coexistence have regularly led to disaster. Only through market economy principles has there been partial success in reaching a new level en route to a better society, in connection with the Enlightenment and democracy (partial because, even in the best organised western democracies, not everything goes well, and because the status quo is also constantly disputed and endangered).

Here the huge development in productivity, which is arguably only conceivable on the basis of the above mechanisms, is of critical importance. Managing a deficiency must inevitably always lead to resentment, frustrations, cultural rejection, disasters, wars. Only when work can be organised in such a way that abundant fruit can be harvested is it also possible to achieve beneficial developments and cultural advancement. From this perspective, the action of the invisible hand in a society that is organised on the western model is seen as an important pre-condition for a high level of culture to be achieved and maintained, or as a factor which plays an important role in this.

However, at the same time, the currently dominant model of the market-based society carries considerable risks, which should now be looked at in more detail.

4.2 The risks of the market economy

Risk 1 – Market mechanisms are getting out of control

One of the biggest problems may be that in principle market mechanisms develop their effect like laws of nature and, per se, they are not aware of any humanity. They do not ask how many human beings they serve and how many they harm at the same time. This is why it is definitely not the right path to assign to these mechanisms a redemptive power that they do not have. Instead it is essential to always consider these as being embedded in the context in which they should develop their effect, and to ask how they should be regulated so that this development occurs to the benefit of as many people as possible. This means, in particular, that the supremacy of the human AA over market laws may never be jeopardised. The effect produced can only be assessed through human awareness – e. g. through that of the voter, the politician, government officials, company employees, company bosses, members of boards of directors, members of civil society, citizens – in relation to their humanity. Therefore it is completely wrong, when considering how much human beings' freedom of decision or how much the effect of market mechanisms should be regulated, to place the balance too much on the regulation of human freedom of decision and design.

First of all this raises the question of to what extent the human being, human awareness, the aesthetic side of the pyramid of needs, human culture, do indeed have due supremacy over cold, intrinsically inhuman, market mechanisms.

Risk 2 – Erosion of political pluralism and democracy

Assuming that Risk 1 is not acute, there is however the immediate question of to what extent human society is engaged in assessment and influence. The second major risk of capitalism consists in the fact that only a more or less limited number of people are given the opportunity to exert an influence. Here there should be no discussion about how citizens can benefit from the fruits of the market system in a balanced way – that is another theme which will be looked at further below –; instead it should first be about how broadly the opportunity for influence is distributed. This question is answered in several ways.

First and foremost it concerns the question of whether the political system follows democratic rules which also actually work and enable everyone to exert influence on politics. In principle two kinds of limited democracy should be considered – with one kind of constraint, democratic rules, human rights and the rules on the division of powers are quite openly trampled underfoot, while the other kind is about all forms of hidden influence such as, for example, through lobbying or corrup tion.

Furthermore, it is about questions such as press freedom, religious freedom, about the question of how social life can be influenced via trade unions, NGOs, civil society initiatives, the culture of protest, which corporate culture prevails in the individual companies and institutions, and how distinctively education, art and culture are anchored in society. It is about to what extent the climate in society is characterised by pluralism. There can only be a form of society with a human face if it is possible for citizens to continue to play a part at all levels.

These themes are in this respect so closely associated with the question of capitalism because financial resources and in particular big business play a particular role in this.

Risk 3 – Unfair distribution

The third major risk of capitalism consists in the question of fair distribution. How far is it possible for all citizens to share in results which are produced through high productivity and scientific-technical progress? To what extent does every citizen receive a fair share, to what extent is there equality of opportunity?

Quite clearly, it is one of the basic principles of capitalism that there is in fact no equal distribution of prosperity. Instead it seems to be an implicit boundary condition that, through commitment, skill, hard work or similar virtues, but also in part in relation to character flaws, considerable material advantages can be achieved and these can also be handed down. Furthermore, one of the basic principles seems to be that once wealth has been achieved, this automatically brings with it a privileged starting point when developing the privileges of the future.

Risk 4 – Consumption mania and resource-intensive growth

Here the question concerns whether the following characteristics of the capitalist market economy dominate social life too much:

There is a distinct drive towards growth and increasingly short product cycles. Events are characterised by marketing offensives, an increase in the moral deterioration of products and planned obsolescence. Consumption of material goods and the question of material wealth is the most important projection field for higher needs. Appreciation, abilities and culture take on a secondary role. The system only functions on the basis of a high level of resource wastage. The understanding that happiness does not particularly depend on material goods and material prosperity and that it is clever to preserve resources in nature, does not have the importance it should be given in the social value system.

Have these risks occurred?

Yes, the continually occurring risks of all the categories mentioned contribute towards the capitalist society appearing to be remarkably suspect.

Risk 1,

i.e. that market mechanisms are getting out of control, is clearly emerging today in western countries. In a society that is characterised by neoliberalism, the supremacy of human awareness, the aesthetic side of the pyramid of needs and human culture over market rules, is challenged to a great extent. Market mechanisms do not function so that they are useful for the balanced fulfilment of needs at a social level, but instead they have got out of control, as cold, inhuman principles with an extremely dubious overall balance.

In this regard the current European and Anglo-American financial crisis is a new height of impertinence. In the context of the compulsion for enrichment which is inherent in the system, the financial crisis has created a gigantic financial bubble with the character of a black hole, which threatens to engulf a large part of the real economic world. The system that is so diseased draws all the attention and all the resources that are available towards itself – with the side effect that the needs of normal citizens, and above all the real misery in the world, here become a fortiori a marginal phenomenon and are carelessly increased.

With risk 2,

i.e. the risk of the erosion of political pluralism and democracy, there are many kinds of harm, but mainly also those that are closely related to the emphasised importance of the monetary sphere of society in capitalism.

This starts with the characteristics of **money**, that its **provenance is not traceable** and it is not obvious in what way – "clean" or "dirty" – it was earned. In capitalism respect for money and capital is particularly high. From this it follows that the area of conflict which motivates corruption and crime has a particularly great chance of having an effect.

Second, the principle of **profit maximisation**, in relation to the increased **hunger for resources** of the prosperous capitalist society, and with the global supremacy of the large powers, leads to big business having priority in all regions in which a profit is to be made. Here the rule applies that healthy markets, political pluralism and human rights have subordinate importance compared to the "hardships" of capitalism, which result from its sensitive position vis-a-vis resource shortages. This pressure also results in random vast capital flows in directions which can be characterised by concepts such as despotism, dictatorship, oligarchy, oppression, exploitation, indifference to human rights, corruption, crime etc., rather than by political pluralism and democracy. Here we can talk about the betrayal of human rights on a broad front, which seamlessly lines up with the crime of colonialism.

Thirdly, in capitalism, particularly if it is characterised by neoliberalism, a real **"professionalism trap"** arises from the trend towards professionalism and the professionalism barrier. If one takes as a starting point the thesis described above of the trend to professionalism (see section 3.9. "The professionalism trend and its side effects"), so the awareness gained by humanity may largely follow the trend of the objectives specified by influential social circles, as the professional path towards awareness is primarily achieved by a substantial effort, sanctioned by influential groups. Ideally, i. e. in a model democracy, the people share prominently in this influence, as a granter of mandates for politicians. However in real capitalism, possibly characterised by neoliberalism, there is a great danger that this determining factor of social relationships gets into a poorly adjusted situation in two ways. First, there is an overwhelming influence by the monetary side. Second, large corporations and geostrategic efforts by the major powers here play a particularly prominent role. In this way, the bulk of innovative efforts mainly result from financial means, which are applied strategically by large corporations and major powers to consolidate their supremacy. So knowledge becomes a factor of power, instead of a basis for culture. There is a great risk that in almost no social field is it possible to avoid the massive implications which emanate from capital and the principle of its proliferation. This relationship has many different forms. Lobbying, studies that are bought, contract and military research, the consulting scene etc. are aspects which represent this principle in a comparatively transparent way. Apart from that, the compulsions to take action, caused by globalisation and neoliberalism, relationship networks of influential people and in particular stakeholders with sufficient capital, as well as a more or less subtle form of corruption, are likely to contribute in such a way that political approaches seem to follow strange rules that do not always serve the interests of the community.

Risk 3,

i. e. the risk of unfair distribution, is the characteristic of capitalism which was the most controversial from the beginning. This risk occurs constantly and instead one can talk about a basic principle that is inherent to the system.

That risk 4,

i.e. the risk of consumption mania and resource-intensive growth, has occurred and continues to be cultivated in the globalisation process at an increased rate is obvious. In the western part of the contemporary world, pronounced and wasteful consumer behaviour is dictated by the market economy and its values, and other cultural aspects thus take a back seat. This characterisation results in the primary purpose of the consumer society being located in level 4A of the pyramid of needs established in section 2.11: "Material and aesthetic side of the world of human needs". The pyramid of needs of a pronounced consumer society therefore has a somewhat distorted focus. Cell 4A, with material individual needs, is accorded a disproportionately high importance. Other levels, which in balanced relationships must in fact be seen as higher goals – such as esteem and recognition (4B), as well as development of talent, self-fulfilment and the promotion of culture and welfare (5B), carve out a comparatively miserable existence. With some irony the pyramid of needs of a consumer society can be described as follows:

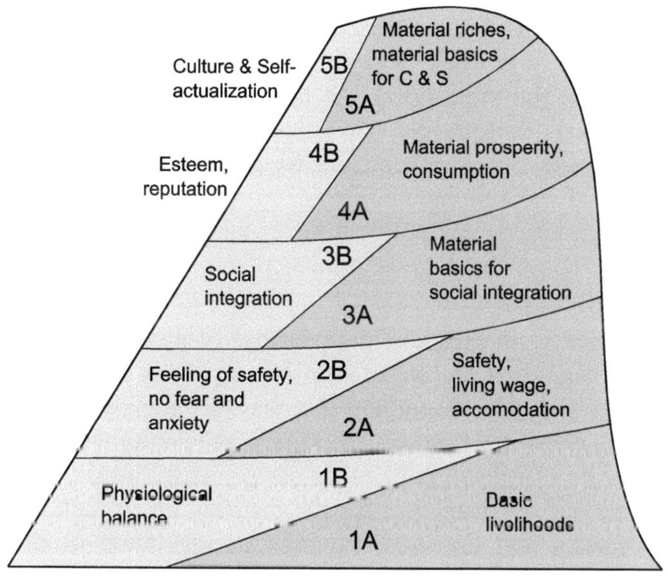

Figure 7 – Pyramid of needs of consumer society

If one follows this thesis this does not, then, mean that capitalism, the market economy and consumption are bad and it would be better to abolish this form of society in favour of another. That would certainly be an incorrect, rather overhasty conclusion. In fact, market competition has an important function, namely that of adequately occupying level 4A of the pyramid of needs and of ensuring that this level is strongly developed enough to be able to be sustained as a basis for the levels above and therefore also – metaphorically speaking – the levels which are a burden on these.

If one looks at the political and cultural setting in advanced countries of the western world, it can therefore be stated that education, culture and solidarity are important issues, which are constantly agonised over. So there can be no talk of a consumer society in its pure form. On the other hand, the thesis of the market as a panacea is consistently shown great respect, privatisations are favoured as strategies for solutions to problems of social institutions, neoliberalism, promoted by influential economic and political forces and not least also by voters, has exerted great influence since the demise of the Eastern Bloc.

Apparently, all facets of the pyramid of needs are definitely found in the social life. No aspect is really unknown and there is nothing that was not already argued about. Apparently, however, no real balance prevails on the scale of values. Political forces primarily wear themselves out by struggling for the distribution of material prosperity and the most extensive deregulation of the market economy possible. That is the major issue that polarises. Even if it is primarily about other issues – such as culture, education, solidarity, humanistic design of living conditions on the earth etc. –, the political discourse likes to focus on items in levels 4A and 5A, as if the provision of basic material needs and the economic system were all that has to be done – anything else will turn out alright.

One can state that the social life functions in a way other than is presented in the political world view of the western model. The dominant ideals do not really satisfy the attained complexity of our society. The prevailing belief in large parts of society and above all in influential circles in the market economy, the consumer society and the leading role of economic growth in the creation and safeguarding of democracy and prosperity should for a long time no longer have dominated political awareness. However, one struggles with the necessary expansion of the horizon.

A drastic side effect of this error is also the conflict between globalisation actors and those countries, regions and cultures on which the market economy is imposed, without providing for equality of opportunity. The protagonists of the world of the western market economy are always very convinced that the expansion of their area of influence will in principle also lead to an expansion of the blessings of prosperity and democracy. Where this does not occur, there are enough explanations for any delays.

In reality it should not be forgotten here that the pronounced materialistic attitude[5] of western policies, from the viewpoint of other cultures, cannot be perceived as well-balanced. For example, a culture with Buddhist or Islamic traditions must deal with the question of how it can adjust to the blessings and consequences of scien-

[5] Materialism is here meant in the sense of market orientation, not in the sense of the philosophical school of the same name.

tific-technical progress and capitalist globalisation. At the same time, however, there is the problem that they are better able to understand the discrepancy that the overvaluation of material prosperity and consumption in the western world has partly assumed an excessive dimension.

That must of course lead to problems of acceptance, as long as western society itself is not able to reflect this situation in an adequate way.

Below, the four risks are examined in more detail.

4.3 Unfair distribution (risk 3)

Arguments against capitalism are generally primarily aimed at risk 3, i. e. the risk of unfair distribution. This approach is however directed against the principle of the operation of the invisible hand, to which the enormous growth in productivity and prominent prosperity observed in many western-oriented countries must especially be attributed.

In fact, one cannot have the one without the other. The law of supply and demand can only work if the market is allowed to develop its dynamic. This includes suppliers having the freedom to set their prices, and consumers the freedom to decide from whom they buy goods and services, at what price. This also includes legal ownership and the sovereignty of market participants, as well as the assurance that profits can be made, as well as the obligation that losses should be borne. In principal it is not wrong to regulate the market within certain limits, but it can only develop its impact if it is also generally accepted that there could be unequal outcomes for market participants.

The acceptance of inequality is also in line with the differential functional principle of the neural system and the principle that stimulus and motivations only arise from the perception of differences that exist between the desired and the actual fulfilment of needs, at least temporarily. So the invisible hand is not only aware of linking self-interest – which is, indeed, necessary because every person is responsible for him or herself – in a synergetic way with usefulness for society, but it also does this according to the functional principle of the stimulus system, which is given to human beings as part of the neural system. The price is the acceptance of inequality, competition, tension.

In principle it is also not negative to allow a suitable dynamic in human society. It would be a utopia and an illusion if one were to believe that a species that is produced by the dynamic of evolution could now completely escape from these principles. However, it is a question of humanity with regard to which spheres, with which resources and in which limits this dynamic is evolving. It is precisely the neural system that enables humans to relocate that which, in the animal kingdom, still seems largely to occur as a struggle for survival[6] to higher levels of emotion and needs. In principle it would be possible for extreme competition to rage within society without even one human being having to suffer damage to life, limb and his mental structure. That this is no utopia, but in certain limits an achievable state, can already be deduced in the conditions in a few advanced, affluent countries. That contradictions in society are perceived as drastic and that differences and the right course to abol-

[6] This perception is also increasingly relativised as part of research into the animal kingdom.

ish these are fiercely debated is here rather a symbol for a suitable high culture, if it occurs in compliance with human rights, basic democratic rules and sufficient social and legal norms.

If one considers the observations on the trend towards subtlety (see section 3.4), then the result is that emotional potential can also have a great impact if the real inequalities are to become increasingly small. From this point of view, the actual opportunities for humanity lie not in equality, but in the subtlety trend. From this one can conclude that it is no contradiction to on the one hand combat inequality and, on the other, to accept and include its impact in the social dynamic at the same time.

In principle it is also not wrong to permit extreme wealth and to allow for the fact that there can be gradual or relative poverty. On poverty it should be said that, from the demand to apply humanism, culture and the aesthetics principle, the demand must be derived to create conditions under which no-one, as far as possible, must forfeit basic livelihoods and participation in social life, under which educational opportunities are open to everybody, under which humans who get into difficult circumstances are given opportunities for support and the path to an upward movement is maintained. However, it must be taken into account that also through one human right, namely that of being able to lead a self-determined life, there will always be life stories that appear to be regrettable. Added to this is the fact that it is not possible to sanction criminal careers without offending the honest section of the population.

From the cultural-aesthetic viewpoint, the difference between poor and rich (in the sense of the material-monetary sphere) is likewise deplorable, but with slightly different focuses.

That there are people who scarcely have a real opportunity to organise their life in such a way that the basic needs can be fulfilled, and for whom the path to participating in the cultural and material wealth of society is scarcely open, is from this perspective not acceptable in principle. This does not mean that abolition or the most equal distribution of wealth possible (in the sense of communism) would be a solution. The acceptance of material wealth is instead sensible in terms of the differential principle of the neural system as a motivation mechanism. However, it depends on the following conditions:

- Social exchange processes must as far as possible be organised so that all citizens have the opportunity to participate, if they try to do this seriously, and that it is possible for them to at least fulfil basic needs in all circumstances.
- The standards that prevail in society must at least consider the cultural-aesthetic aspect and its precedence over the material-monetary aspect to such an extent that it appears to be extremely absurd to regard material wealth as the highest factor of power; that instead it seems self-evident to treat material wealth with due responsibility – in terms of the rule: "Money and wealth, no matter how large, have no importance at all for image and reputation. The importance of these informational values can only arise from the way in which wealth is dealt with."

The result is a desirable distribution of material wealth with a broad foundation – according to the principle: "There is as far as possible no absolute poverty any more" – and that, building on this, wealth exists in distribution of any kind, but this is unlimited

A not unimportant aspect here is the need for no-one to be disconnected from the market and its offers. Poverty of the individual should, as much as possible, only go so far as to exist in a class of population that represents market power, so that it is profitable for companies to serve this market. On the other hand, it is also an ethical requirement that marginal groups should also explicitly participate in the market.

The concept of fair distribution suggests that this kind of fairness can be achieved through redistribution. That is not completely wrong. However, the relevant strategy can only function if it is primarily aimed at the demand to strengthen the performance of the market system, while at the same time removing anti-pluralistic mismatches and considering the primacy of cultural values, as described in the other sections. Only to the extent that this path is successful can and must the state ensure that basic disadvantages, and in particular living conditions that exclude, are abolished.

From a cultural-aesthetic point of view, however, fair distribution primarily also means the urgent need for capitalist economic activity and the exploitation of resources in poor regions of the world to only be permitted if the basic deficiencies of food, health and education there are eliminated and economic conditions are designed in such a way that regional entrepreneurship can develop on a national sovereign basis for the good of the population who live there.

From the cultural-aesthetic point of view, the concern is mainly to provide the system of social vitality systems so extensively with interfaces that all citizens have enough opportunities to link their individual vitality system to these. Redistribution is only an alternative strategy for the gaps which, due to the failure of this causal therapy, cannot be closed from a material viewpoint. Material redistribution is urgently needed, but at the same time it is also clear that cultural cooperation cannot be achieved with this strategy alone.

From this perspective it is more obvious to use the concept of the sufficiency of the vitality system instead of that of fair distribution. Sufficiency of the vitality system implies the demand for fair distribution, but on the whole this is about much more far-reaching demands. A society can, then, be described as to some degree fair if the individual vitality systems of all members, as well as the vitality systems which are in all social spheres, form a complete system that provides all those involved with sufficient opportunities to fulfil their needs at all levels of the pyramid of needs.

4.4 Communism's misguided path

In fact communism no longer plays a role. The following digression is needed, though, to clarify that the aesthetics principle has nothing to do with left ideology.

From the perspective represented here, it is absolutely necessary for a form of community to be advocated in which – as for example in communism (or also in socialism) – the notion of fairness plays a prominent role. With regard to important basic theses and the familiar attempts at implementation, communism and Marxism are however to be regarded as an aberration.

First, this is also just a special form of envy complex. Criticism and attacks against capitalism occur in the material-monetary sphere. Wealth and private ownership of the means of production are demonised. No serious attempt to break out from the cycle of material economic thinking and counter-thinking is discernible. Also, from the position of poverty, it has not been possible to escape the fascination exerted by wealth.

Second, the baby is being thrown out with the bath water. The economic potential of the law of supply and demand is negated and the abolition of the invisible hand is one of the core beliefs of the concept of communism. In principle it is noted that impetuses result from contradictions. With regard to the contradictions, which can lead to high productivity, it is however apparently not possible to obtain a practical approach from this knowledge.

Third, dogma and force are part of the concept. The dictatorship of the proletariat should be established through a revolution. The sequence of social order is in theory extrapolated into the future, without taking adequate notice of the fact that new systems are always built on the advantages that are part of existing systems. So the development of feudalism led via trade, which was encouraged by colonialism, to mercantilism, which again prepared the way for the capitalist market economy. The idea to continue this evolutionary process through dogma – the dogma of the abolition of private ownership of the means of production, could have gone badly, but with today's knowledge of history it is clearly easier to see through than in the early capitalist era.

Fourth, the perception is increasingly focused on the material-monetary sphere. Historical materialism, relating to the economy, to which Marxism is bound, leaves no room for discussing idealistic, dualistic or creative perceptions that transcend such positions.

What is regrettable in this is that, through the tribulations of the communist experiment, the impression was fostered that there is no alternative to a market economy that is characterised by Wall Street capitalism. Thus the religious absolute supremacy of the market principle, which today, with its neo-liberal tribulations, does so much harm, has now become possible.

4.5 Consumption mania and resource-intensive growth (risk 4)

The shift in society from prioritising the perfection of consumption demands to prioritising the perfection of cultural requirements should not have the potential to endanger economic prosperity. Quite the contrary, new types of demands are always the most suitable for encouraging social exchanges. This could be beneficial for all kinds of markets, cultural interexchange processes as well as material-monetary markets. But what hopefully can result should be a shift in the social exchange towards immaterial values – precisely this aspect strengthens the hope that the problem of shrinking global resources can indeed be resolved.

But this is only a realistic prospect if a drastic shift in values takes place. Characteristics of the western kind of market economy, like planned obsolescence, the acceleration of fashion and consumption cycles, as well as the throw-away society, are inconsistent with various aesthetic requirements. These tendencies can certainly not be negated completely if the principles of the market economy are still affirmed. But the challenge is to find a healthy balance in this regard, which is today a long way away.

The affluent society is deeply characterised by a competition of vanity and greed for new products, money and wealth. In correlation with these demands, the cycles in private and business life are constantly accelerating; markets are always geared towards increasing sales and profits, reacting very sensitively if this does not occur. The state is expected to support the steady growth in material prosperity for all. The result for those involved is often more of a hamster wheel effect than a certain feeling of fulfilment and happiness. In this respect, developments in which these kinds of processes accelerate less quickly can actually improve the scope for lives to develop in a more fortunate manner.

The solution for the problem of gigantic waste dumps and environmental damage left by the consumer society should not only be sought in better recycling technologies, but also, and especially, by avoidance. That is only achievable by a more subtle and sophisticated handling of material resources.

A particularly difficult problem for affluent societies is that incentives for a more conscious and subtle lifestyle exist in principle, but these are systematically kept away from consumers, so that they are not deterred from constantly increasing consumption by rationality. All products are presented in neat and beautiful packaging. And how much environmental devastation is involved, how many adults or even children are exploited, and whose health is damaged, who are left in poverty, misery and famine, how much water and other resources are wasted, is not visible. And waste dumps are carefully kept away from the niches of affluence – by avoiding clues about the negative consequences and environmental damage that is caused in far-off countries.

It is mainly a problem of perception. Some facts about the misery in the world and about the disastrous way in which the environment and resources are handled leak out, but consumption is faster and its evocative character reduces the possibility of pausing for a moment, or of having scruples.

This kind of self-deception, in the present conditions, is completely intolerable from the aesthetic point of view.

The circumstances in which everybody is able to meet the challenges of life can be reflected by a system of coordinates, with special attention given to the four quadrants, as follows. The y-axis describes the achieved level of gratification of needs, and the x-axis views humans' wisdom and cleverness as having a precautionary intention, as the owner of the natural mandate, to determine how global human society is arranged and developed. Regarding the y-axis, it is assumed that circumstances where ambitions mainly focus on overcoming

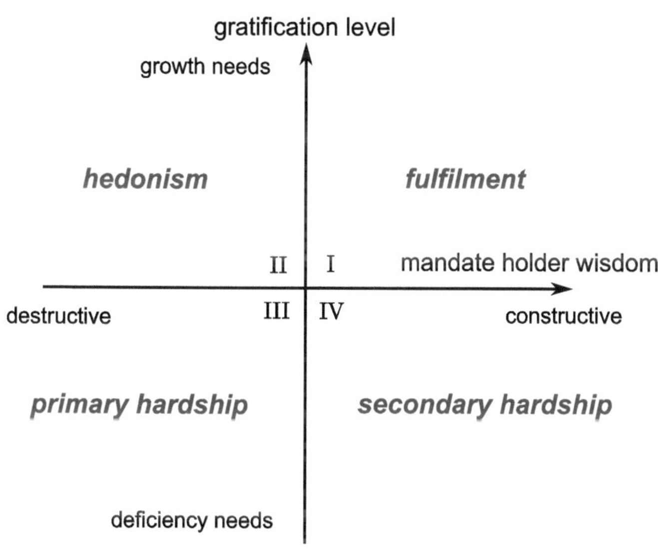

Figure 8 – Needs and mandate holder wisdom

shortages apply to the negative range of the y-axis, and those where the needs for growth dominate are primarily in the positive range. With the human wisdom x-axis of the system of coordinates, it is assumed that attitudes and behaviour can be classified as positive if they are suitable contributions to one's own future, to the future of one's own family, and to the future of cultural succession.

Humans living under any kind of conditions of hardship, or who have to regularly fight against such hardship, most likely belong to quadrant III in the system of coordinates. A person who exhausts himself as much as possible by fighting deficiencies will normally hardly be able to think about his own future or the future of his descendants to any major degree. Thus the assumption is that humans, living in such circumstances, will rarely be able to occupy quadrant IV.

If there is a way which leads to quadrant IV, then this is probably via preliminary journeys through the world of growth needs, via a certain strength of gratification, a certain sense of basic trust – with the help of skills which support the ability to keep one's head high, even in conditions of deprivation. A typical reason for moving from quadrant I into quadrant IV might be provided by health issues, either unexpected or age-related.

However, it is more interesting to consider the growth aspect of the y-axis. Humans who are able to develop growth needs and express these most likely have the choice of whether to cultivate these in a constructive manner – in the sense of the future, of succession, legacy – or not. It is assumed that it is rather part of human nature to be inclined to be discerning and clever about the future and about legacy. It is believed that successful socialisation in a society, with a certain level of education, freedom and prosperity, typically leads from quadrant III into quadrant I. There may be detours through quadrant II, but fulfilment is finally achieved in quadrant I. We should state that by far the vast majority of people would opt for quadrant I, if able to choose.

What the consumer society makes of it is as follows. A beautiful-looking carpet is spread out before the people, covered in many products of the affluent society, and it is suggested that this is the right sphere of activity for growth needs to be expressed. Of course, the portfolio is also enriched by real cultural accomplishments – like art, knowledge, education, good behaviour, ethics, law and order etc. – but the material-monetary aspect of life is encouraged by product marketing, and also by marketing of cultural achievements as products. The natural growth ambitions of citizens who are freed from immediate deficiency needs are channelled and the horizons are closely defined.

The effect of this artifice is finally that the level of hedonism is reached in society which is required to keep the growth spiral of the capitalist marketing machinery running properly. The people believe that they are in the right precautionary mode. Happiness in life and a sustainable succession are mainly sought by having as much money as possible; this is not completely wrong, but it is at best only half the story. It is acceptable to disregard, harm or destroy cultural-aesthetic values in the name of shareholder value because of a certain overestimation of the material-monetary aspect. Precautionary concerns are one of the most important motivations; but human action due to noble motives, which is halted halfway, in reality degenerates to hedonism.

It is not true that the behaviour of citizens in affluent western countries has to be broadly categorised in this regard. Instead there are massive attempts to resist the belief in the blessings of capitalism; and there are reasons why neo-liberalism is very controversial. But the core values are still aligned in such a way that the deception of market participants about the real cost, and particularly about the cultural-aesthetic implications, is explicitly accepted as inherent to the system. This kind of desired manipulation leads to a notable level of human motivation potential, originally targeted to quadrant I, in fact being redirected to quadrant II, in order to serve shareholder value. In the end this is a convenient self-deception at the level of society as a whole.

Continuing with this view, it is argued that one of the characteristics of the consumer society is that there are many people who would prefer to head towards quadrant I, but who yield to the temptations of the market economy to a certain extent, resulting in hedonistic weaknesses, which in fact brings them nearer to quadrant II than probably they would like.

This sounds harmless, and in relation to a single person it is in fact harmless, but because of the consequences for society as a whole, livelihoods will largely be destroyed if an appreciable shift in values is not introduced in time. The widespread misbehaviour at the same time provokes changes, making the shift in values inevitable. The remaining question is simply how much irreversible damage still has to be done, before the mankind organism reacts appropriately.

Summarising, one could say that those human beings who live in cultural or material poverty have little opportunity to influence mankind's fate, and that those people living in affluence are, statistically, too comfortable to do so, whereupon the consumer society is used as a comfortable vehicle to head towards the abyss, happily and carefree.

It is important to take note of this trend and to strengthen efforts to avert it sufficiently seriously. On closer examination it is observable that the shift in values started long ago – there are many indications of this. But the pack as a whole is still running in the wrong direction, because the crude belief in the blessings of the market economy is still too deeply rooted in society.

Chapter 2.12 ("Pyramid of needs and vitality system") considers, amongst other things, that humans are inclined to understand the social and natural environment of the human being, the impact made on this by action, and the implications for the individual vitality system. The thesis is that humans tend to recognise certain areas regarding the environment and society, and the impact apparently caused, as relevant for their vitality system. It is an ultimate principle of marketing strategies that they are aiming to minimise or form these areas, which in this respect are seen as relevant. The exact opposite would be the right approach – the desire to create maximum transparency.

In relation to the topic "needs and mandate holder wisdom" (figure 8), it is again important to mention that crisis situations are particularly fraught with the risk of getting out of control, because the possibilities in quadrant I are decreasing significantly. The opportunities to achieve fulfilment are partially lost, or people are even pushed into secondary hardship (quadrant IV). At the same time, prospects for young people to socialise by developing growth needs and by occupying quadrant I to a sufficient extent are reduced. A domino effect might be caused, resulting in the collapse of essential parts of the social vitality system.

4.6 Erosion of political pluralism and democracy (risk 2)

Freedom of choice at all levels, a distribution of political influence that is as balanced as possible, and the active participation of all citizens in social processes and in material and cultural goods, achievements and accomplishments, are basic requirements. Here it is also particularly important to consider human society in the world as a whole. Here the function of the market economy and its participants is to place themselves in the service of a beneficial development of the global cultural society.

What really happens today is in blatant contradiction to these requirements.

The capitalist and globalising society, sustained by the glorification of material wealth and the machinery of marketing, encourages the appearance of behaviour that strongly favours destructive actions such as crime and corruption, whereby again efforts to construct social processes in such a way that values like fairness, justice and legal certainty have a good chance are undermined.

In addition, large corporations, banks and oligarchies that operate multinationally have many opportunities to successfully defy democratically controlled regulation and continued legitimisation by the consumer in a pluralistic, evolutionary process sustained by competition. What is characteristic about this is that, inter alia, they also achieve this by exerting significant influence on political decisions. Not least, in the more recent history of the world there are thus many processes in which the decisive influence has been characterised by a capitalist compulsion to maximise profits and the constantly increasing demand for resources. As far as possible, international groups operate unchallenged on the international scene and in doing so play national political powers off against each other. There are no democratic political forces at a global level[7] and nation states are stuck in the game of supremacy on the global markets. This means that large corporations gain a political importance that they are not in fact entitled to.

In the end, this is related to the fact that capitalist society, including large corporations, is desired by many citizens, voters and consumers. However, at the same time, an inclination to certain excesses is observed, which definitely go far beyond what may be in the interests of the majority of citizens, which again is expressed in a certain political disenchantment, in a growing lack of trust in the proximity of politics to the people in many advanced democracies.

This can be explained, not only through the political importance of internationally active large corporations, but also through relations within more influential classes of the population, through lobby work, through corrupt and criminal influences on politics, through a lack of transparency, through the professionalism trap and through deregulation, which have led to large corporations and banks being able to focus on monetary and political potential, which as such effectively represents a constant potential for blackmail for society.

In order to give pluralism and democracy better opportunities it is therefore sensible to place particular emphasis on the following requirements:

- The context in which companies can develop must be adequately regulated. That is only satisfied, in

[7] The UN is at best to be regarded as a precursor to such global political power.

particular, if companies no longer have the opportunity to reach a size and strength of financial resources that lead to any kind of relevance for the system. It cannot be permitted that the compulsion to rescue it derives from the hole which a private company could potentially tear in the social structure. In order to confront this problem at least two approaches are possible and they should, also, both be used. First, with the risk of a certain critical size of company, a certain level of market control, there can be intervention – e. g. through antitrust proceedings. Second, the system can be enlarged. For example a global political system would be more able to confront the bankruptcy of a large corporation or a large bank with compensation measures that show solidarity towards the employees, savers or business partners concerned, than can an individual state. Essentially it is about not harming certain proportions between maximum company size and minimum state size, as well as between the maximum market presence of a company and the minimum counter presence of its competitors. These are not new demands, but this concerns quite basic experiences which the capitalist system at a national level has already made common, and the necessary countermeasures are well-known. Precisely because of the fact that such all too well-known rules at a global level are once again quite clearly violated, at the same time an important affront against democratically-formed social relations derives from the capitalist principle of performance.

- The breeding ground for crime and corruption must be curtailed. That such kinds of actions are in any case not endorsed morally by social norms, and that they are penalised, is thus regarded as a precondition. For more details on this see below in section 5.3: "Crime, corruption and mafia structures".

- The professionalism trap must be noted and its mechanisms must be adequately respected. Naturally, the trend that in all social spheres there is an increasingly high level of professionalisation is irreversible and on the one hand it is of almost existential importance here that humanity consistently finds a way out from the mounting technical, economic and ecological problems. However, it is equally important that, on the one hand, stimuli from the whole of society flow into this process, and on the other hand, that the issue of global social development is processed in a target-oriented and unconditional way in an open discourse.
- The former can only result from a largely open and pluralistically organised society, based on the virtues of the Enlightenment, democratic constitutions and legal systems, human rights, freedom of thought and press freedom, equal rights and equality of opportunity, as well as transparency and cooperation between social classes, spheres and professions. Regarding this aspect, there are extreme differences worldwide and there is no lack of reasonably positive examples.
- The second, just as decisive, aspect is examined further in section 5.6: "Short-sightedness of democracy and the professionalism trap".

Of course, the demand for establishing and protecting a balanced equilibrium between companies and democratically legitimised political systems also applies in the opposite direction. A state with a disproportionately pronounced inclination towards regulation and with excessive bureaucracy can only result in the entrepreneurial dynamic grinding to a halt. Here particular care should also be taken that companies are dealt with appropriately, according to their size. Bureaucratic constraints which a large corporation can meet without significant commercial relevance using a department set up specifically may be inclined to paralyse a smaller company.

When establishing democratically legitimised global institutions or a global political system for the purpose of creating an appropriate democratically legitimised opposition to large corporations, care should be taken to observe the relevant focus. What is definitely not needed is a global bureaucracy that works against national and regional civil identity and development. This conflict also already exists between nation states, which are partly federal states, and regional governments, and the cultural-aesthetic perspective is quite clearly related to the demand to encourage a diversity of regional identities, just as the variety of cultural identities of minorities is an important asset.

4.7 Market mechanisms are getting out of control (risk 1)

Securities trading and **speculation** have the important function for the economy of spreading risks. It is clear that the modern economy would not function without this spreading of risks. So that this activity can fulfil its function, there must of course be the right incentives, which consist of allowing profits to be made and retained. However, this does not mean that this market should be freed from all shackles and that it should be allowed to lift itself off the ground of real values in an increasingly extreme way, in unlimited profit maximisation hysteria, and to expose the global finance and economic system to the danger that it may be ruined again by speculation in increasingly large amounts. An important requirement is to regulate this system in such a way that it reliably fulfils its function, but that it does not put at risk any other cultural achievements. Derivatives should be put under scrutiny in both a detailed and more general way. Containment of high-frequency trading through minimum transaction charges (such as for example the Tobin tax), could limit the trend towards the increasing virtualisation of traded securities. Every other idea on how securities trading can be transferred to a reliable mode that serves the development of culture is welcome.

In particular, the **banking system** has the function of securing the necessary capital for the economy and administering savings and loans for the public. The banks' field of activity should be regulated in such a way that they fulfil their function reliably, but so that the financial system cannot be put at risk, and that they cannot evade responsibility for their failures.

Commercial enterprises have the function of providing the material foundations for prosperity and culture and giving the public a platform for participation in social exchange processes. For this to happen it is definitely right to aspire to the highest productivity possible and to constantly increase this in competition. The **stock market** has the function of providing capital for companies and giving natural persons and institutions the opportunity to participate in commercial successes, or alternatively to jointly assume responsibility for failures. The general framework for companies and stock markets must be formulated in such a way that they can fulfil their function, but at the same time ensure that no unnecessary harm and risks result for cultural society and the environment. In particular, the following parameters must be observed:

- Shareholder value should never have priority over cultural values, within which the integrity of the environment once again has an intrinsically special value.
- It must be ensured that the power, influence and potential for blackmail of a company can never be greater than the influence which is in effect exerted through the democratically legitimised legislative and executive. This point was already discussed in the previous section.
- Fair competition in all sectors must be guaranteed and the market must not be controlled by monopolies or oligopolies. In principle this is about the economic dimension of cartel law (above it was more about its political dimension). In any case, competition must be given priority over the maximisation of shareholder value and productivity. If an excessively powerful large corporation dictates prices and thereby increases its shareholders' profits at the expense of consumers, then the neoliberal formula used for this, that this is also a legitimate way to increase consumer welfare, must be resolutely rejected. Pluralism and freedom of choice for consumers are in any case a higher good in terms of a cultural society than any strategies to maximise profits, productivity, gross national product or any other arbitrary parameters of achievement. The economy must be regulated in such a way that companies are dependent on continued legitimisation through free

consumer decisions and they never achieve a status which allows them to direct or even control politics.

Finally, there is a close relationship between economic and political plurality. In the previous section, the demand for a balanced constellation of power between state and company was highlighted. This demand also applies in relation to the major players in the financial sector. The regular caving in of governments in the face of the potential for blackmail, which is provided by a few particularly liberally constructed financial centres, is not acceptable. If the Tobin tax or other measures that may be seen by the public as being reasonably defined are not enforceable because a few players do not cooperate, then a democratically legitimised global institution must be established that has sufficient powers at its disposal to enforce these measures. It is certainly not wrong to also continue to allow some competition between financial service providers and financial centres, but not at the cost of a roulette game by high finance and an extreme imbalance in relation to fair taxation.

The assumption that large corporations can organise trading and production more efficiently than smaller companies may be partly true. However, another part of the truth is that they tend to establish a supply chain with high margins between producers and final consumers, that they also regularly use the available space to establish nontransparent technologies that inflict harm on employees, consumers or the environment, and that they try to use databases and information processes in a way that allows them to strengthen and expand their market positions. It cannot be good if large corporations are allowed to do what they want in this regard with no criticism or challenge. If it is possible for a company to either successfully conceal practices that are questionable from a cultural point of view or, despite disclosure, to retain these without significantly harming its position in the market, then this is a clear indication that the break-up of this company for cartel reasons is overdue.

It is not about suffocating the financial sector, large industry and other powerful institutions or tycoons, or removing the room for manoeuvre that they need in order to operate successfully, but it is about ensuring a balanced constellation of power and stability, which offers the real opportunity, using democratic means, to develop a global cultural society that is really worthy of the name.

Incidentally, corporate culture is also part of human culture. That there is a corporate culture at all and that it complies with modern standards should become self-evident. This applies to external behaviour as much as to the culture in the company. That is definitely not a new demand; as already mentioned above, there have long been appropriate models, e. g. under the designation Corporate Social Responsibility (CSR). In some firms there is already a good atmosphere without having to first launch major programmes or invent eye-catching descriptions.

The market economy-capitalist organised society is and always was characterised by the constant struggle for the compatibility of market laws and other cultural demands. Fundamentally it has always been clear that, beyond Mammon and the glorification of wealth, marketing and self-marketing, there are also other parameters that influence social life. However, it can be assumed that the prominent belief in the material-monetary aspect was and is decisive in a particular way for the most recent period of history. It depends on identifying imbalances and learning how, at all levels of social life, capitalist mechanisms can be assigned to their correct position.

4.8 *The neurasthenia of economic growth*

Modern capitalism with a trend towards deregulation is characterised by the following features, amongst others:

- Greed for increasingly extreme profits largely prevails as a positive model. Almost every means is acceptable to follow this model – until it is retracted, i. e. until there is harm or a crisis situation and this leads to storms of protest.
- The motivations are essentially aimed at short-term profits. A sustainable increase in prosperity, fairly distributed opportunities to participate, as well as the sustainable development of a particular shareholder value, will either be categorised as not necessary or simply as being goals that are less important. Similarly, the attitude to all cultural and legal values is established.[8] With regard to profit-making, it is sufficient in a standard case if at any time a change to investments is possible which again promise to generate profits in the short term.
- Protagonists of shareholder value do not largely care how capital is increased, the main thing is that it is increased. There are no questions about whether there are real values behind the numerical values, whether they are based on a financial and monetary system that will develop in the long term in a

[8] However, that is no dogma but a trend, from which there is also regularly a partial divergence in relation to marketing motivations, Corporate Social Responsibility and humanistic behaviour of significant personalities.

healthy and stable way, whether the whole thing develops as a pure financial bubble or a pyramid scheme or not.

- It is left to the states to use measures to regularly ensure that the global financial system and the global economic system can continue to develop in a stable way. At the same time, state policies are steered in a direction with a partly increasing emphasis that robs them of the opportunities to effectively oppose crisis-ridden developments.
- In democratically-led political systems, short legislative periods lead to short-sighted politics. The public tend to succumb to the prosperity principle, the temptations of the consumer society, and also, in particular, the regular gifts made by policies. A policy of constant benefits which develop in good economic conditions becomes an existential diktat in times of crisis.
- While it is normally sensible to treat financial risks with appropriate risk awareness, as well as to provide some scope and reserves for uncertainties, households and investments are increasingly subject to pressure for bonuses and benefits, they are largely exhausted and risks are obscured and ignored. This applies to the economic activity of states just as much as that of large corporations and institutions in the financial world. To plan ahead for the next crisis in good economic times or, with public debt, to consider the risk of increasing interest rates, is not so appropriate. Instead the opportunities are exhausted until nothing works any more.
- Crisis is forever. Because of the self-imposed pressure to constantly maximise profits and prosperity

when applying all risks the whole system is constantly in a highly nervous state. Moderate stock exchange weaknesses, moderate slumps in growth make market participants and market regulators tremble and they are always inclined to submit to a corresponding compulsion to act. The system imagines that it is often ill, or at least in great danger. It behaves like a patient that needs help and calls for intensive care and attention.

The latter is the real scandal. The western economic and financial system is constantly focusing on itself in an intensive way. While – seen from a distance – it is extraordinarily powerful, and fluctuations in terms of services provided tend to be marginal, this system takes itself and occasional minimum downturns in growth extremely seriously, immerses itself in dreadful narcissism and in this respect it is always inclined to draw events in the world into its spell.

The following is another characteristic:

- The pressure for growth increasingly occurs completely divorced from economic reality in the form of an excessive system of virtual values. This characteristic would still be excusable if this numbers game were to take place in a closed area – according to the principle: "investment bankers like to have their fun." Unfortunately, however, it is the case that failures in this game are regularly passed on to real economic life.

So the second scandal consists of the fact that, through this game of virtualisation, the danger is constantly growing that utopian commitments come up against the real economy, national budget and taxpayers, which no longer have anything to do with real life and real achievements, but which threaten to eliminate these as a minor matter. The scandal here is, in particular, that it is not the protagonists of Wall Street capitalism and such established economic and financial systems who accept responsibility with the seriousness required, but the tax-paying public and people who are dependent on social security benefits, pension funds or savings. For the protagonists it is more a sort of failure that can also of course be dramatised, but for the public it is an existential problem and for society it is about the risk of an unprecedented descent into poverty, radicalisation and war as a consequence of a far-reaching financial and economic crisis.

While this game is played with the risk of the destruction of already existing prosperity, there are enough focal points in the world that are characterised by poverty, massive deprivation at the low levels of the pyramid of needs, cultural upheavals, hardship, infirmity, epidemics, war. These focal points partly exist in the middle of the affluent society or between the subsidiaries of financially strong companies, but also in places which tend to be a long way away from global economic affairs.

An important function of the capitalist economic system must also be to address these focal points, in particular, in terms of the development of global culture. What happens is largely the exact opposite – the differences with these focal points are stirred up in the name of shareholder value and demand for resources and the risk that new focal points emerge is tacitly accepted.

In particular, the necessary requirements are as follows:

- Strong economic activity must become the norm. The short-term maximisation of profits, the bonuses of investment bankers and the consumer welfare of people who already live in the affluent society are acceptable principles of motivation, but these must always be less important than risk management aimed at future security.

- The system of the globalising capitalist market economy should not be allowed to contemplate its own navel but it must be placed at the service of the cultural development of the whole of humanity. It is clearly necessary to continue to support the achievements of the market-based system – but not simply as an end in itself and because of the fun that a few representatives of the human species can have with wealth, but to maximise the opportunities to develop a comprehensive global cultural society. The specific material wealth of a few exotic characters must not be an object of envy, as long as this does not prevent the possibility that every human being has the opportunity to participate in the cultural wealth of the global population, which naturally implies the possible fulfilment of basic needs, as well as a certain room to manoeuvre and development opportunities.

It is also important to ask the question of negative growth. Negative growth is always a normal event, both in the economic or even global, as well as in the structural, sense. However, until now it has always been accompanied by the destructive development of the psyche and of living conditions and is one of the greatest fears of the market-based society. A society that is sufficiently well established must, however, be able to also deal with this case in a well-calculated way, and in the sense of cultural-aesthetically accentuated fair distribution.

A particular issue would be that of the cultural and informational growth in the competence of society during simultaneous negative growth, particularly in the market for resource-intensive consumption. The ability to deal with this issue may be the decisive factor in future demands.

4.9 Crisis management and deregulation

It is quite sobering to have to watch the kind of crisis management that is usually practised today. A crisis always represents an emergency situation, with extreme pressure to act. But it does not demonstrate wisdom if the debate is focused on following or avoiding the pressures, each of which are urgent, especially not if, by using suitable manoeuvres, the outline of the future is organised in an inadvertent, rather than in a targeted, way.

An important requirement would be to partly disengage oneself from the overheated debate, to search in an analytical way for the causes of negative trends in development, to clarify how, on the basis of new knowledge, the right solution and the right action plan could have been defined – and from there, to look for a compromise solution that may, though, still go close to the aim that is defined in this way. On the question of what should happen to Europe, it would be sensible to develop different alternative concepts and to submit these to the voters.

In Europe, the crisis that began in 2008 is, amongst other things, accompanied by rekindling the discussion on the right method of how the appropriate parameters of the market-based system are to be regulated.

Keynesianism?

Definitely, as long as there is no model that offers a more sophisticated solution for the cyclical aspect of the economy. But for this the appropriate room for manoeuvre required must first, once again, be created. If the states are so over-indebted that they are already overwhelmed by this burden, the question of boosting the economy through public debt is no longer asked.

Monetarism?

Definitely, as long as there is no model that offers a more sophisticated solution for the inflationary aspect. But for this the appropriate room for manoeuvre required must first, once again, be created. If however there are extreme pressures to minimise interest rates and to print new money in large amounts in order to avoid a fatal contraction of the capital market, the question of controlling growth in the money supply via tightening interest rates is no longer asked.

Further deregulation?

Definitely! Above the demand was made for the extreme regulation of some parameters at global level, as well as the break-up of large international corporations, monopolies and oligopolies, the introduction of transaction fees, regulation of the financial market and the prevention of financial bubbles that loom all too large over the real economy. In addition, it was pointed out that it is the wrong approach if one looks for the solution for all social problems in privatisation and deregulation, it depends much more on allowing the cultural aspects of life to have priority over commercial aspects. In this regard, however, the conclusion should not be drawn that any liberalism and any deregulation is to be demonised. A real economy that is characterised by pluralism, competition and true freedom of choice is essentially the part of the economy that is suitable to really serve the cause of culture. So this part of the economy must continue to be protected and promoted. The trend towards growing criticism of neoliberalism should not result in the mistake of classifying liberal attitudes exclusively as negative. It is much more about regulating activities in a targeted way, where it proves to be necessary. If, because of fear of the main sources of misery, global oligopolies and states with pretensions to be great powers, only the symptoms are combated using regulations and bureaucracy, this is the exact opposite of what should be done. Regulatory measures are appropriate, then, if one keeps a close eye on the major actors, in particular, who have the potential to jeopardise the balance, and to grant smaller players, who are already relatively harmlessly integrated into competition, optimal conditions.

What else?

Yes, all progressive economic theories are welcome. However, what is essential is that they should be applied with a sense of proportion, an absolute awareness of risk and respect for all members of society, without exception, and that the approaches are first and foremost determined by awareness of creating and preserving the necessary room for manoeuvre.

Further deepening of the debt morass, further cash injections by the central banks, a further increase in virtual financial market bubbles?

One cannot absolutely deny these developments in principle if it is about rescuing social harmony. However, it would be important to state here how much society is hooked on the drug of unfunded liabilities and how much it requires suitable therapy.

5 Disaster or culture?

5.1 On the question of cultural development

This book does not go into greater detail about what culture is, according to which laws the cultural-aesthetic sphere is developing, and which rules may have to be observed within this sphere so that successful development can take place. Here, as a priority, attention should first turn to the greatest inconsistencies, which are to be deplored because of contempt for relationships between the cultural and material spheres of society across the globe.

As stated above, it is assumed that human society as a whole has a natural aspiration to climb the pyramid of needs. So the development of culture, as well as its variety and quality, is a process which consequently occurs with the collaboration of all human beings, if it is possible to oppose the worst crises and cases of destructiveness. For this reason it is particularly important to examine why world affairs continue to be characterised by a multiplicity of disastrous events, and how this trend can be contained. If clarity prevails in this respect it is also sensible to question how to deal with wealth and prosperity.

5.2 Bureaucracy, regulation mania and creativity

This section does, however, provide a small discourse on a few questions that are asked as part of the development of culture in the affluent society.

In the first chapter, it was pointed out that bureaucracy, regulation mania and the pedantic, petty, restrictive organisation of social processes makes humans ill or slows down creativity. Basically, though, it is normal that in society mindsets show a certain range between pedantry and creativity, and that life is characterised by this contradiction. Both are needed – observing certain rules and the persistent eradication of tasks that may tend to be less stimulating and varied, as well as the creative and artistic interaction with life. There are people who are suited to bookkeeping and others who are true artists. The truth lies in the ambivalence between both mindsets. Furthermore, jobs also arise from the demand for pedantry and the petty regulation of life, which is ultimately better than unemployment. However, this trend is a shackle for the development of a cultural life. If, in the world of rules and laws, a 'special rule for a special rule' is created for the thousandth time, if the excessive number of dots over the 'i's is apparently growing faster than the know-how of humanity, if it is quite rare for a simplification of the bureaucratic rules to be made possible, then in the end this is a massive obstacle to a fruitful structural change and to human happiness.

In order to solve this range of problems it would be necessary to consider at least the following two cases:

- There are processes that are made complicated for objective reasons. In this regard ways must be found to cope with this and to master the necessary balancing act between conscientiousness and adequate psychophysical health.
- There are processes that are unnecessarily artificially complicated. In this respect there must be clarification of why this happens and how this trend can be countered.

In the latter case the approach could be for the continuing naive iterative increase in regulations and laws to be replaced by their deliberate organisation and a focused design. One of the most important design rules here could be simplicity.

In relation to the first case, i. e. the demand to acquire knowledge about the correct approach to the inevitable requirements of complexity, a few hypotheses can be gained from the aesthetics-paradigm:

What is the cause of depression?

That organic or genetic dispositions can play a role in depression is not examined here. Only the psychic configuration will be examined.

Depression results from the fact that the moments of stimulation in the AA that are differentially active are weakened or reversed. During the development of depression a high level of activity is needed in order to obtain minor positive assessment stimuli. If eventually it is no longer possible to obtain significant positive stimuli despite the high level of activity, the basis for the stimulus collapses. In the view of fellow human beings, the person concerned may still have “functioned”, but in his own world view the activities no longer bring him any improvement, but nothing other than new problems.

Manic-depressive disorders result from the attempt to once again initiate the differential stimulus by desperately setting a focus. For a time this happens with astonishing success, at the price of instinctive aimless activity. Eventually, however, the resulting distorted perception is overtaken by the need for realism and the house of cards collapses.

With the phenomenon of burn-out it is not clear what may be understood by this, but a certain closeness to the concept of depression and so to the hypothesis described above can be assumed.

How can the phenomenon of attention deficit disorder (ADD) be explained?

Here this is also about a vague concept. However, it is at least clear that it concerns a problem that is related to a lack of concentration. To explain this phenomenon there are two hypotheses from the aesthetic paradigm.

First it is about the physiologically-determined balance of power between the complex neural mechanism on perception and control, on the one side, and the dirigiste demand of the AA, on the other. If the connections and processes of the AA are developed comparatively more weakly or more strongly in relation to sensory and motor signal processing in the cerebral cortex, then the result is a lower or a higher ability for concentration. So it can be assumed that there is a certain range in the genetically and ontogenetically determined configuration of the brain that have an effect on the ability to concentrate. Here the question of which of the configurations is better or worse cannot be answered, since it is neither possible nor acceptable to define a standard for this. At best the question can be answered about which configuration is better adapted to which environmental conditions; if the environmental conditions are created by humans, the problem is reduced to the question of why those members of society who are apparently less well adapted are not sufficiently involved in the creative processes.

Second, it is about the relationship between human beings in relation to their different understanding of aesthetics and the awfulness effect. Here it is no longer only about considering the question of an absolute or abstract ability to concentrate, but the question is raised of which kind of perception makes concentration more or less possible. For the sake of convenience one can proceed from the model of two humans who both have the same absolute ability to concentrate and the same level of fitness and daily condition. As part of real perception and thought processes, however, both will always be able to concentrate in different ways, because each brain reacts differently to a specific content. This means that both humans have a different taste.

In this context the question of conformity with the environment still has a significantly higher importance than the phenomenon of an absolute ability to concentrate. Here it is about which aesthetic feeling has affected the environment and how the aesthetic feeling of a particular person is related to this. The greater the respective difference, the greater also the resulting awfulness effect. From a certain aesthetic skill with a certain profile the result is a certain tendency towards rejection in the perception of information from surroundings that do not meet the relevant taste. The stronger this automatic defensive reaction, inevitably the lower must be the ability to concentrate on the subject of perception.

Essentially this is about the great advantage of the human being who is equipped with the AA, that all thought and perception processes are automatically filtered. Normally, this configuration serves the purpose that aesthetic taste avoids concentrating on contradictory offers, or that it regards these critically. However, in the largely restrictively-formed process of education and work in modern western society this advantage conflicts with reality. In relation to the pronounced aesthetic skills there is a high potential for conflict with regard to the required level of adaptation.

So the lack of the ability to concentrate could be caused by both:

- a physiological configuration of the brain that is a disadvantage in relation to specific requirements, or
- a configuration with an aesthetic experience that is too skilled or too little adapted to the social context.

The drama is that up to now the latter aspect of the ADD problem has tended to be noticed reluctantly or at least not with due attention, that ADD is first and foremost regarded as a kind of illness and a problem of adaptation and it is left to recommendations to those who are suffering to learn how they can better adapt to the demands. Here this phenomenon may also be a clear sign of a distinct creative potential that is available in society but which unfortunately is largely wasted.

The idea that this only concerns the possibility of better adaptation is only conditionally productive, because here it is about pronounced system incompatibilities. The patterns of thought that develop in a young person may anticipate particular demands that must be mastered in the future. These patterns of thought could conflict with common patterns of thought. Essentially it is part of the normal socialisation process to also learn to connect the relevant aesthetics incompatibilities. At the same time, however, the reserves of power available for this are limited, so that a temporary resource-related antagonism grows.

It would be important to at least subject this second hypothesis on the theme of ADD to a test. One cannot, however, in any way deduce from the belief that this hypothesis is correct that the work process and education must be entirely placed at the service of creativity. It is much more the case that the work process always also involves routine work that is to some degree perceived as mindless at each level. Living together consists of adaptation and compromises. For the education system it is true that specific demands, rules and the content of learning, even if these are perhaps questioned, nevertheless have a value, because they can teach the necessary ability to adapt and to persevere.

How is it possible to master complex demands?

In fact the answer to this has been known for a long time: through the possibility for self-determined actions and control over events. Studies have shown that company bosses master complex demands with significantly less stress than their closest subordinates because they normally have more control over events. Of course this also includes the fact that there are prospects for the future for which the efforts could pay off.

The opportunity to be able to act in the educational and work process in a largely self-determined and fearless way is, incidentally, also a possible solution for part of the ADD problem that has long been undisputed. In this regard it is also important to find the right balance between freedom and social need.

Here, once again, the circle on the theme of excessive bureaucracy and regulation is closed. If regulation mania and bureaucratic pedantry are not halted in a targeted way, the chances for achievement, health and creativity are poor. Here the development opportunities for society must be seen as a higher good than those for bureaucrats. This also applies to economic policy, where the regulation of a few essential boundary conditions, in particular at the global level, could be the basis for preserving and creating a lot of free space (see the comments in Chapter 4: "Culture and market economy", in particular section 4.9: "Crisis management and deregulation").

What about the tendency towards addiction?

Addictions result from techniques needed to improve the differential overall balance of processes that are operating in the AA. Actively coping with life's demands is only possible if, at the end of the day, the week, the month, a positive balance of feelings is achieved. Otherwise the stimulus dries up and depression results. This positive balance is essentially based on the following preconditions:

- Fulfilment in terms of self-actualisation or in terms of level 5B of the pyramid of needs or in terms of quadrant I in figure 8 – Needs and mandate holder wisdom. For fulfilment in this sense belief, of whatever kind, can make an important contribution.
- Mental techniques and tactical balance management. This happens through the conscious or unconscious, but usually targeted, setting of emphases in terms of any needs at any level of the pyramid of needs.

The second aspect plays just as important a role as the first. However, if the former falls behind too much, then the result of this is the growing dependence on tactical focuses and therefore the tendency towards addiction.

Analogous actions at the level of society as a whole are the "further deepening of the debt morass", "further cash injections by the central banks" and "a further increase in virtual financial market bubbles" (see also section 4.9: "Crisis management and deregulation").

How are age-related loss of brain performance and dementia disorders understood?

Initially, it is clearly proven that there is a connection between the ageing process and loss of brain performance. Dementia disorders are growing mainly because people are always getting older. But are we completely helpless in the face of this phenomenon? Apart from age there can be quite different influencing factors for this kind of loss, such as for example genetic makeup, organic illnesses, infections, latent poisoning, traumatic experiences, psychological crises etc. Therefore it is very largely outside the scope of a human being to influence his fate in this regard. Probably, however, a few of the actions have something to do with the fact that the AA is weakening and, amongst other things, the following factors could also be responsible for this:

- Performance demands decrease. In particular there is a tendency that the demand to constantly learn and adapt oneself flexibly to new situations declines with age or that there is a decreasingly objective need to organise life dynamically. Here there is also a connection with gradually reducing physiological resources and the correspondingly increasing limitation in the space available for an active way of life. Furthermore, a certain degree of experience and sedateness leads to fewer mistakes being made and fewer risks being taken. So the AA may have to achieve less and less in the later stages of life and its processes and structures tend towards partial atrophy.

- The preconditions that are needed for optimum performance of the brain, the memory and the AA not only have something to do with demands, but also with the question of whether it is possible to regularly shift the AA into a pleasure-oriented work mode. This is only possible on the basis of enough sleep, the opportunity to be able to occasionally give free rein to fantasy, the ability to include playful elements in the life plan, the opportunity to be able to experience hopes and successes. Obstacles are in particular pressures to perform, in terms of the human being and the brain having to function, as well as boundary conditions that lead to mental impairment and depressive incidents, and a lack of foundations for fulfilling basic needs.

To maintain the efficiency of the neural system, it is also best to live life to the full for as long as possible and to actively organise this life in order to climb the ladder of needs as far as possible in the direction of growth needs. The monetary-material aspect of the pyramid of needs certainly has the disadvantage here that it leads to a reduction in the demands placed on the AA, while a fulfilment in terms of the aesthetics principle and self-actualisation does tend to involve more favourable boundary conditions for maintaining the efficiency of the neural system.

What about the Internet?

In many respects the Internet is a great facility. The technical principles of Internet communication are based on concepts that were made far from dedicated commercial interests. They already specify that all participants can use the resources provided on an equal footing. The combination of packet-oriented information transmission and non-deterministic routing creates technical boundary conditions that normally do not allow the transfer of information to be filtered, channelled or monitored.

So until now the Internet has been able to render a valuable service to society. Inter alia, some human beings who are exposed to informational oppression – which frequently occurs in relation to other kinds of oppression –, nevertheless have certain opportunities for communication. Amongst other things, this forms a highly effective counterpart to the trend towards professionalism since every participant, irrespective of his or her importance in the social structure, can provide content. It is also essential that there is no distinction in Internet communications between rich and poor, because technical boundary conditions mean that (some) commercial participants are forced to make investments from which all other participants also benefit.

However, current developments are leading to fears that this brilliant plan would increasingly degenerate into a romantic idea that is undermined by reality. So using totalitarian methods it is even possible to gain control over communication flows, to a certain extent – e. g. by providers (or alternatively also other holders of key positions) being under an obligation to the state or by tapping all gateways, switches, routers, cables, Internet exchange points which connect the infrastructure to be monitored with the rest of the Internet. A further possible method of control consists of making access to the Internet difficult or not even allowing this.

Even if one were to leave the opportunities for control to one side, there are enough other unattractive aspects to Internet use that could still be mentioned. So in many offers there is some truth that users' personal data or information on the user is collected and marketed. It is in principle obvious that this data should serve as raw material for a commercial manipulation machine, and, for example, for it to emerge again in the form of personalised advertising. Moreover, what happens to this data and to what extent basic civil rights remain protected in this regard is often less transparent.

Another problem is Internet crime, which grows all the more the greater the importance of the Internet is for society.

In future relations with the Internet it would be important to preserve the basic idea of open and equal communication as much as possible. For this, civil liberties and data security must be strengthened and legal solutions must be created that do not disadvantage network operators too much compared with other commercial participants.

It would be important to preserve the great platform for understanding that the Internet can be or could be as much as possible so that any unsophisticated contact with this is risk-free. Only then can it serve international understanding to the degree that is needed.

5.3 Crime, corruption and mafia structures

Apparently there are at least two important reasons why crime, corruption and mafia structures can grow like a cancer.

The first reason is to be found in poverty – in the fact that many human beings live in precarious or degrading circumstances, that important basic needs cannot be satisfied, that there is no access to satisfactory education, that opportunities to take part legally in market development and the cultural wealth of society are not adequately provided. As is known, that is a suitable breeding ground for criminal energy to develop.

The second important reason is the opportunity for anonymous participation in processes of social exchange. A typical opportunity for this is provided by money as a means of anonymous exchange. In addition there is a range of opportunities for concealed actions, whether as a (uniformed) member of an army or militia, as a masked participant in a demonstration, as an anonymous telephone stalker or as an anonymous blogger or troll in the Internet. In particular, the anonymity of money again gives society the opportunity for the basest instincts to be able to gain ground at a high and at the highest level.

In order to minimise the breeding ground for crime that was mentioned initially, i. e. that of poverty, the basic cultural and material problems in society in all regions, classes and castes in the world have to be solved. For this it is essential that those members of the population who have the good luck to be able to indulge in the needs for growth extend a hand to their fellow human beings and open the way to equal participation in all market-based and cultural processes. Here market-based elements are certainly an important basis for a positive development but not, though, if they are allowed to get out of control and become the highest principle, but only if it is possible to regulate them and to place them in the service of the upwards development of culture throughout the world.

With the second important reason for crime, corruption and mafia structures, the situation is less clear-cut. Some of the opportunities for anonymous actions can be limited by the legislator if necessary – it is no accident, for example, that in Germany there is a ban on wearing masks in demonstrations. With other opportunities – for example in the Internet – the increased focus on secure identities requires technological progress as well as a certain change in culture. As part of money laundering legislation, anti-corruption laws, tax legislation, criminal law etc., bank transactions can be monitored in a limited way. But, besides this, currencies are only of use to society with the required efficiency if transfers and investment management do without petty monitoring and without the abolition of bank secrecy. With cash, however, the limit is finally reached. Here freedom, as well as anonymity (relating to provenance and destination) form part of the implicit rationale. With prohibitions and restrictions it is, if anything, impossible to achieve a far-reaching solution to the problem of anonymity.

However, perhaps it is also possible, through positive thinking, to arrive at a method of resolution. In by far the majority of cases, action in the social context is linked to the fact that one has to answer for the consequences. The relevant balance is expressed in the reputation and in the image that one can enjoy in the social environment. That applies to natural persons just as much as to institutions and firms. It is no accident that image building is very important for firms who are competing. It is indisputable that informational components such as know-how, patents and image have a higher significance than the capital base. Therefore after a bankruptcy, a corporate image that has been developed for decades or centuries can still successfully be sold. Finally, this also expresses the fact that aesthetic-cultural-informational values and processes take precedence over the material-monetary sphere.

It is known from sociological research that human beings are always then almost automatically inclined towards honourable behaviour if they assume that they may be observed, and that egotistical behaviour patterns may only have an opportunity in secret, in supposed safe obscurity. From the history of mafia structures, drug cartels, colonial conquests and Hitler's fascism, it can in turn be concluded that this strange kind of obscurity can, as part of a radicalisation of society, infiltrate the social system of values, if one assumes that neither judiciary nor progressive social forces, which are concerned with humanity, might be present as an effective counterpart.

From this knowledge of the boundary conditions of human action it can be concluded that it must be beneficial for the desire for a humanistic configuration of society if values like reputation and image have a particularly high significance. Essentially, as stated, such a high status of values in society is rather natural. However, in this regard there is a certain scope for variation that exerts a vital influence on the opportunities that exist in society to disseminate unfair, corrupt, criminal behaviour.

In order to allow integrity to have better opportunities it is therefore sensible to emphasise the following demands in particular:

- In all social spheres, great value should be placed on transparency, reputation and image. These values may be the most important cornerstones of the cultural society.
- Only acting under one's own, reliable (e. g. in the Internet) proven identity and authorisation can have a value in society. Anonymous actions must be prevented through legislation, order and sufficient technical solutions in areas in which there can be negative effects.
- Money and wealth, however great, have no importance at all for image and reputation. Importance

for this informational value can only grow from the method of handling wealth.

- At the same time, it is extremely important to ensure through the legal system that control over money and wealth cannot be achieved through dishonest means. Fighting crime, corruption, tax evasion etc. is one of the most important social concerns. We can only talk about a cultural society if it is possible to successfully highlight these values. In theory this seems to be largely undeniable, but in fact there is no region in the world that one could describe as having completely successfully implemented this desire. Fairer tax at the global level can only be achieved by establishing a democratically legitimised world state or an institution that is adequately equipped with executive and judiciary power in this regard.
- Primacy of the cultural-aesthetic sphere over the material-monetary sphere of society must be expressed, inter alia, by any attempts to buy image points using financial means being exposed and rectified as such as far as possible by using an appropriate form of perception. If, for example, adverts launched by large corporations are not regarded with the scepticism required, this point cannot be satisfied.
- It is extremely important to foster the sensitive handling of processes that build reputations.
- Anonymously expressed statements and anonymously diffused information can generally have no influence at all on reputation-building processes. The assumption that it is possible to effectively follow this principle in all areas of society hardly

seems realistic. On the other hand, however, it must be clear that any deviations must lead to unfairness and the accumulation of destructive potential.

- Respectful and courteous interaction with every fellow human being and with his or her opportunity to show himself/herself as a human must be a generally respected social value. Bullying and slander are criminal actions.
- Reputation is an important basic human right. The legal system must incorporate a dedicated law on reputation.
- The system of the social vitality systems must be developed and optimised in such a way that citizens have sufficient interfaces to integrate their individual vitality systems into legal processes and structures. Here it is about cultural cooperation, jobs, balanced distributed education and career opportunities, artistic, business, scientific, charitable, activist, political, family opportunities to develop etc. and about respectfully interacting, without exception, with every member of society.

If image and reputation in society have a high value, money is not confused with reputation, the rule of the primacy of cultural-aesthetic values over material-monetary values is not harmed, the cultural society continues to develop and the system identity of individual and social vitality is sufficiently observed, it can be assumed that this is also thus linked to containing crime and corruption.

In addition, it should also be mentioned that of course a legal system that is based on ethical values and the will and ability to also assert this is an important implicit boundary condition for an appropriate upward trend.

5.4 Environmental destruction, waste of resources, population explosion

The fact that human beings try to use nuclear power, that by doing so they risk nuclear contamination that is inimical to life in entire regions, that has already happened in part and will most certainly happen again, that they create a problem of nuclear waste etc., is on the one hand completely irrational and, on the other, it also conflicts with any kind of motivation that would be justifiable in relation to a reasonably healthy emotional dynamic. The only possible explanation for such behaviour can be that human beings, if they act in this way, believe that they are in a serious emergency situation and that they no longer see any other way out.

However, in societies that use nuclear power it is not obvious that there is a real, serious need. It is much more the case that they have simply committed themselves to principles (such as, for example, the compulsion to consume and to a much higher level of comfort), that ultimately lead to decisions where adherence to these principles is dictated, not by any emergency, but instead by an easy adherence to the path once taken. From this perspective the use of nuclear power is only one of many signs that indicate that in its behaviour, human society does at least have a tendency towards insanity, to put it mildly.

From the aesthetic viewpoint this is particularly striking.

Other extreme symptoms are wars and terrorist acts of destruction, as well as any form of violence and repression. This will be examined in more detail below.

Apart from this there are many other puzzling aspects that, perhaps with a slightly lower level of absurdity, do however take the same line in principle. These include, amongst others – as described in Chapter 1:

- the burning of large amounts of fossil fuels resulting in a rise in the greenhouse effect and sea levels, shifts in climate zones, an increase in extreme weather events, the accelerated erosion of mountains etc.,
- the blight of the landscape by wind power plants and high voltage power lines,
- the decimation of natural biodiversity as part of cut-throat competition and the creation of artificial diversity using comparatively amateurish methods,
- the destruction of the environment through waste, contamination, monocultures, forest clearance, urban sprawl,
- the promotion of scientific-technical progress with a crass disrespect for balance, synergies and symbiosis, whose development has taken entire epochs and the effect of which must be regarded as the essential basis for life,
- the extreme exploitation of all resources, which somehow are technologically usable with no consideration for the consequences for humans and for nature.

All these trends obtain their special importance through the following two factors:

- Scientific-technical progress provides humans with the possibility to achieve all these crimes in an increasingly efficient way.
- The explosive increase in population ensures that humanity can also drive this process to the furthest global borders.

Humanity is heading directly and in a scarcely restrained way towards the widespread destruction of the environment and the source of life and to the final collapse of the economy.

The fact that the price of important resources like food and oil is intermittently increased so much by speculation that this results in critical conditions and great hardship throughout the world is an initial, still relatively weak symptom of this expected development. The call to contain speculation, particularly in relation to food derivatives, is certainly right and worth considering. The hope that the problem can finally be solved in this way alone is, however, not justifiable. The fact that the appetite for resources of cars and the oil industry already conflicts with the need to feed the global population is alarming.

Climate change, with the expected consequences that are already gradually occurring and are no longer to be denied, is another absurdity.

From the viewpoint of a reasonably sound rationality, but also from the viewpoint of the aesthetics-principle, these trends can only be described as completely disastrous. On the one hand, planet earth is full of clever people who are able to assess special circumstances with a high degree of competence and seriousness, solve the most complex problems and successfully conclude the most expensive projects. On the other hand, society as a whole acts in such an irrational, unintelligent way and in profound opposition to the feelings and demands of its members.

Basically there are the following explanations for this phenomenon:

- The exaggeration of consumer mania.

- The professionalism trap.
- In general the fact that for a long time the human being has no longer had any natural enemies, apart from himself, that he has therefore retained full responsibility for his actions but is reluctant to adjust to this fact. He spreads himself about almost like a cancer that threatens to eliminate its host and therefore itself, where, in comparison to cancer, he does not seem to behave in a significantly more intelligent way.

The avalanche of problems that is rolling towards humanity is so dramatic that escape is only possible if all opportunities are used. This also, without fail, means the further intensification of current efforts towards energy efficient and ecological economic activity. Further important requirements are, however, a clear reduction in the trend towards expansionary resource-based consumer behaviour and the containment of population growth.

The former would require a shift in values, an adjustment of the scope for growth needs, in which the material-monetary sphere as a primary focus loses importance and instead information, knowledge, art, reputation gain in significance. This implies that it should be linked to the trend towards higher regard for cultural values and the integrity of the environment. It would also be right to talk here about a contraction of the markets for resource-intensively produced products and a limitation to what is necessary. The horror of this vision for nervous capitalist markets may be contained if one is inclined to notice that the growth in exchange processes is merely shifted to another level. On the one hand, these are quite common cultural exchange processes, on the other this also results in a lot of new demands for the world of products, as for the world of finance. Until now, aesthetics was also already one of the most important factors driving the market economy and the advertising industry is particularly keen to use this leverage. What is changing significantly is only the direction in which the ship is steering, not its destruction. It is not the case that the demands that humans make on culture and the markets are disappearing, or that they are becoming more limited, instead they just change or increase in an as yet perhaps rather unfamiliar direction. This is about nothing more than a special kind of structural change.

The second important demand, that of containing the growth in population, can only be fulfilled if the causes that are responsible for this problem are eliminated as far as possible. This can be expressed quite simply: poverty must be fought resolutely and minimum standards regarding education must be enforced. Education would also include knowledge of the global consequences of a larger number of offspring. Poverty and social uncertainty must at least be combatted to such an extent that applying this knowledge is also actually possible.

Despite the urgent need, an undoubtedly satisfactory global economic performance, and the convincing simplicity of this strategy, it seems infinitely difficult to seriously follow this path. A few important steps have already been taken. For example, the United Nations General Assembly started to enforce the "International Covenant on Economic, Social and Cultural Rights" (ICESCR), also known as the "UN Social Pact" or the "UN Pact I" on 16 December 1966. Unfortunately, however, this initiative, like many humanitarian projects, was purposefully undermined in the power game played by large corporations and great powers (cf. Ziegler 2013, 112ff.).

It would be all the better the quicker the long overdue structural change that is described starts in earnest, and the quicker a global consensus on humanitarian demands can be achieved. Otherwise the day may no longer be far away on which the question "Disaster or Culture?" no longer needs to be asked.

This structural change depends on the behaviour of every human being, on the way he lives his life every day, on his social attitude and on the question of how he exercises and passes on his natural mandate. However, an important clue also lies in particular in the perception of human beings who are involved in the process of drawing up global agreements on dealing with environmental risks. The question is of what kind of mandate they would be given by citizens whom they represent, and to what extent the relevant attitudes are characterised by narrow-mindedness or by vision.

In terms of how the environment is reflected in the neural system, with the fulfilment of needs and the vitality system, the rule applies that only a particular part of the environment can always be regarded as relevant. This field at least always includes direct experience. However, there is a particular expectation that humans will also use their imagination, their memory, their cognitive abilities etc., in order to follow the logic of imagination, the time-related and spatial limits of which go far beyond the immediate environment and current events. Here it does not matter to what extent predictions about dramatic developments will really occur in the future. Instead it is much more about the fact that there will be active management of risks that probably exist according to the best knowledge available. During the negotiations for the follow-up agreement to the Kyoto Protocol, however, one can only state that the future of humanity is being completely gambled away in a narrow-minded poker game of interests and power.

From the cultural-aesthetic viewpoint, it is not acceptable for environmental or cultural values to be damaged by monetary demands without first clarifying the question of how this damage will be compensated. This clarification is needed, since an omission can have unforeseeable consequences. As far as any kind of impact on the environment is concerned, this leads to the need for an adjustment to the burden of proof.

Until now it has fallen to nature, as well as to environmentalists, activists and scientists who are in favour of its protection, to provide proof that there has been damage and that there are risks. The need for action must then be enforced using what are, in part, insufficient resources against the centres of capital and political power before action can eventually be taken, but typically this does not really lead to suitable measures.

A satisfactory solution to this problem has to come from the presumption of guilt and a change in today's still largely upside-down burden of proof. With any impact on the environment it should generally be assumed that damage will be caused and that, in general, with technological and economic activities, proof is required that this damage will be minimised and compensated. This requirement must apply to all global actors, but in particular also to large multinational companies and global powers.

Adjustments to the burden of proof are also offered as a method of resolution with regard to the relationship between the world of capital and wealth on the one hand, and people suffering from destitution in poor countries on the other, as well as concerning the requirement to enable the latter to be adequately integrated into social vitality systems.

5.5 *Striving for power, violence and wars*

The behaviour of humans as social beings and the dynamic of the process of social development is characterised today by great ambivalence. On the one hand there is marked progress in many respects, on the other hand, animalistic behaviour patterns regularly come to light. With each year of evolution this mixture becomes more explosive. This idiosyncrasy of human society may on the one hand appear to be extremely ridiculous – for example, from the perspective of a grain of dust in the universe – but on the other hand it must be extremely worrying – for example from the perspective of any human being who, however, finds himself by chance in a mood in which he is not deluded. Ultimately this peculiarity is, however, both explainable and also preventable.

Let us start with the explanation.

Above, in the section with the identical heading, it has already been established that human beings' historical situation was characterised by the need to assert oneself in a hostile environment and to bring to bear all means available to do this. From the laws of nature it must follow that this also includes the following means, amongst others:

- A demonstration of strength.
- The defence of hunting grounds or territories.
- Violence and homicide.

These patterns of behaviour or of needs are part of a context that features the following characteristics in particular:

- The environment is full of dangers and hostile creatures; it is about naked survival and the assertion of a position in the food chain; the means available to assert oneself in this environment are marginal (once there was a time when the human population was very small).
- The scope for action of groups of people was strictly limited.

The current situation is mostly the exact opposite:

- The means that human beings have available to assert themselves are extreme and increase every year. For a long time man has no longer had any natural enemies (apart from himself) and he has long stood at the top of all food chains.
- In principle there are no longer any territorial limits. There is close integration between all nations, groups and classes. Everything is connected to everything else. Every serious crisis and every slightly more serious infection circulates throughout the entire world. The earth has long been a large shared home for mankind.

The dilemma is that the old patterns of behaviour are still very deep-seated.

Particularly with the individual, but also with nations and social groups, practices have become more sophisticated. However, the inclination to accumulate and provoke hostile feelings and to act out feelings of aggression are present at all times and in all places. For a long time the most important project for the global population has been for the whole of society to climb the pyramid of needs but on the other hand this demand is also constantly denied and betrayed. The hypothesis that, in order to survive, it is necessary to create an area of influence that is determined by territorial or physical dominance which, if necessary, must be defended by all means available, is not likely to vanish from one's mind.

It is a banal truth that this will never finally happen. In fact the reawakening of such hypotheses is always one of the fall-back scenarios if there are problems. This principle results from the historical basis of human society and from the law of the relative prepotency of needs, which is always also applicable to the lower level of needs.

However, the fact that in addition this hypothesis does not disappear from the more or less systematically developed perception of allegedly progressively-minded political and economic forces, and that the majority of the population allows it to happen, must be seen as anachronistic. The demands of a few particularly power-obsessed examples of humanity are widely approved, as long as it seems possible to relate one's own hatred, one's own claim to affluence and wealth, one's own beliefs, to their strategies. Situations in which dissatisfaction grows, whether through crises that occur by chance or through randomly escalating conflicts, regularly lead to an increase in this trend, so that the danger of a downward spiral is always present. In terms of the pyramid of needs, we can regard this in such a way that global politics is always at risk of being massively dragged down by the prepotency of deficiency needs that expands like a major conflagration.

The remedies for this are every form of growth needs and the commitment of the majority and of minds that think and act strategically to the self-fulfilling prophecy that this route to humanistic progress is viable.

Of course it is extremely important to protect the identity and independence of certain groups, ethnicities and nations; from the aesthetic viewpoint this is already also absolutely sensible. Of course, attacks on human rights must be rejected. This probably means that the use of the last resort, that exists in violence or even in war, is never completely eliminated.

If, however, there is something that is definitely not acceptable, then it is the inclination of many groups, large corporations, states and major powers to aspire in a strategic way to the calculation of physical force, the potential for military threat, or blackmail through money and property rights. One of the biggest problems here is the close interdependence between poles of power, in the form of militias, state military and national interest, and the material-monetary poles of power, developed in capitalist market action. The economy and, particularly, large corporations, tend to build strategic alliances with the relevant military and state poles of power. Here capital, state and military power are each involved.

Companies' ambition to be increasingly competitive is only natural. It is normal that plans to achieve a dominant market position are forged in the boardrooms. Companies can be constrained in this ambition only by consumers, competitors and cartel law. However, if these mechanisms fail, then high finance enters into a fatal symbiosis with militarily supported state power. If the market, determined by freedom of choice and pluralism, fails and politics allows the trend towards excessive capital concentration, the state's susceptibility to blackmail by large corporations also ultimately increases. Both are dependent on each other and can do almost nothing other than work hand in hand on creating as much dominance as possible.

To this is added the problem of the resource-intensive nature of economic activity, already discussed above.

Pressures to secure access to resources worldwide result from the hunger for resources, that these days is generated by a powerful and thriving national economy, with the need to systematically utilise both all the options resulting from market action, as well as from the political-military dynamic. The capitalist system, particularly also in relation to the tendency towards the pronounced and consciously forced consumption of material goods, therefore creates an artificial emergency situation that makes geostrategic striving for power the condition for the survival of the system.

It is therefore no wonder if today the global powers, ironically, attract attention for obstructing many essential humanist and ecological initiatives. They are motivated to do this through their self-generated dependence on resources and the possibility to comprehensively exploit these. By concentrating power, both from the material-monetary aspect as well as the military-political aspect, they have the opportunity, by striving for power and advantage, to get by for a time.

What is true of major powers is just as valid for all smaller and, at the global level, less prepotent countries. Unfortunately there are enough examples of the struggle for regional or territorial demands using blackmail, force and war. Capitalism is not always involved.

The state, and ultimately also therefore the large corporations, could only be constrained if citizens make a serious intervention. Major powers and other poles of power could yet get into circumstances in which they are confronted by an alliance of less power-conscious states, gaining more and more strength.

Ultimately everything is a question of the social power system. Its rules are not only true for political relations within a state, but also for global power relations between states. Thus there are at least two power systems within which a major power, a regional power or a dictatorship must continually fight for their particular demands.

It is logical that the global community of states tries to constrain the dominance of the major powers and the folly of militant states and groups. However, what logic could lead the internal power system to want to undermine the claim to power? Why should a nation want to constrain its own government and the military of its own country in its ambition to preserve and expand its status? The answer is quite clear: it does not want to do this. Ultimately it is legitimate to defend one's own needs and one's own strength and therefore also the strength of one's own country. Therefore it is not possible to deny this or to demonise it.

However, what may not be legitimate are the means that are deployed to do this. This therefore means claims to power being asserted in tune with the times and carried out with the appropriate subtlety. And that is a demand whereby citizens living in a country that has claims to power could very well be on equal terms with citizens who also live in this world. Within certain limits concerning the extent of agreement, there could be a situation, on the basis of a shared demand to construct a global cultural society, in which a large number of human beings join together from different nations and classes.

In principle this is a long-standing and gradual process. The demand to create a world that is characterised by humanism, human rights, social protection and peace is a project that has been under way for a long time. Every development in relationships is also always related to the ambition to find an acceptable common denominator which is, though, also always confronted by destructive actions and powers. Humanist demands are anchored in many constitutions. The supremacy of political actions over military ones is the most important rule of global politics.

However, the problem is that the success of this process is time and again fatally questioned, that after political conflicts are partly resolved ultimately, however, these are consistently made worse, and that self-reinforcing processes of destruction gain momentum, clearly showing that, after a promising phase of reconciliation, the next great disaster is in each case pre-programmed.

There is an important problem here deriving from the fact that human beings and society, within the processes of contraction, crises and conflicts, are not simply confronted with the danger of a gradually lower fulfilment of needs, but also with the possible fact that elements of structures or components of the vitality system are questioned that have an important meaning for the entire system. Thus losses that, viewed from outside, may appear insignificant and manageable in fact threaten the system in which human beings have established themselves. The emergent nature of the neural system, the fundamental uniqueness of the mirror of perception in the mind of the individual and the demand for sovereignty of every human and every group that logically follows from this leads to the fact that assessment of the gravity of the consequences of the respective threats only affects those concerned. In conflicts, the almost inevitable consequence of this fact is that one of the parties to the conflict regularly crosses a red line that it cannot see, leading to unexpectedly fierce resistance from the opposing party to the conflict. Any kind of conflict escalation is explained by a lack of attention to this relationship.

Another problem arises from the fact that, inevitably, because of the different position that each player takes in the global scheme of things, because of the different perceptions and the differing living conditions of each player, this must lead to actions that are, on the one hand, to some extent well-meant but the consequences of which, on the other hand, are perceived as negative. Even with the best of intentions (assuming this is the case), this danger is not completely avoidable.

Moreover, what is problematic is that destructive actions are also always linked to the consequence that the convertibility of cultural and material-monetary currency systems is tending to decline. Interpersonal relations are limited or damaged by an increase in antipathy and this leads to a decline in the opportunities to exchange intangible values. Through growing uncertainties and psychological and physical threats, exchange processes lose part of their vibrancy at the most diverse cultural and material levels. Thus in principle the danger increases that essential parts of the vitality system threaten to become unstable.

Furthermore, it must be borne in mind that cultural ties, intellectual skills and other elements of the intangible substance of the vitality system develop little by little, and that this process will only succeed if a certain continuity is at least partly possible, something that concerns material living conditions and peaceful cooperation. This is a development process that requires much more time than economic reconstruction, for example. So a conflict where there is significant hardship can lead to the loss of certain, difficult to replace substantive elements of culture, or prevent their creation.

In order to escape this dilemma, from today's viewpoint it is probably especially important to pursue a path that drastically increases the chances that growth needs can comprehensively determine events in the world. In order to do this, it is especially necessary to impose the following requirements:

- A level of community development should be sought in which all human beings, depending on the mental and physical potential they are given, can, by their own efforts, ensure that their basic needs are fulfilled.
- All human beings must be allowed a fair chance, in which they can participate in cultural processes and achievements.
- If it is not possible for a region, an ethnic group, a class of population to successfully promote the process of integration, based on independence, in the social exchange process, solving this problem has priority over all other social tasks and demands. If extraordinary means are required for this, such as, for example, the temporary protection of a weak regional market through duties, or its possible support through subsidies that are provided from the tax coffers of the democratically legitimate global state, then this has precedence over the otherwise valid principles of the market economy. The fragile seeds of market participation, whose development is, however, the condition for the integration, based on sovereignty, of part of the global population, must be protected until there is a certain ability to compete. This includes not expecting them to have to compete with highly productive or even subsidised large corporations on a level playing field. This in-

cludes support for subsistence farming, irrespective of what productivity has already been achieved, and protection from encroachment by the logic of the market, or by financially strong or corrupt/militant/ criminal forces.

- The growth strategy must be organised in such a way that the entire system of relationships is not deliberately destroyed because it leads to a global lack of resources. In particular, mental growth, education and the development of the intellect offer the best prospects for being able to satisfy this demand. The distortions of the current capitalist system, neoliberal hyperbole and the growth strategy that is decisively geared towards an increase in the consumption of material goods must be overcome or at least weakened in favour of a more cultural-aesthetic direction, as described in the previous sections.
- Ultimately, the character of globalisation must be changed in such a way that less economic dependence and contrariness is fuelled, that instead strategic economic synergies are established for as many people as possible, and the demand for the development of a global cultural and affluent society is communicated in a credible way. However, as long as the decisive winners of globalisation are focused on military and economic dominance and on a priori non-human shareholder value, inevitably this provokes rejection and hatred.
- In relation to potential or apparent conflicts, all sides must be clear that every smallest increase in pressure, every smallest pin-prick can provoke an existential threat (to the vitality system) to those on the receiving end. Thus every threat scenario must

gradually lead to the build-up of pressure which must be released at any time, also if the primary attitude was quite defensive (assuming this is the case). It is a reasonable demand to cultivate the ability to withstand the pressure, without increasing the counterpressure. Only if that is the main strategy does the concept of defence, in whose name military departments today usually operate, not become hypocrisy.

- A relentless embargo policy, even if applied to an especially inhuman regime, can only be wrong, as this mainly affects the people and takes cultural substance from them that later could be the basis for the peaceful organisation of a humanist-democratic society.

Making claims to power with resources that are suitable for this day and age means using intelligent and subtle means, with politics, diplomacy, wisdom, negotiation, as well as with openness and transparent behaviour, not, however, by pitting military or economic strength against each other, with the world being taken over by big business and with the dogma of the free market at any price, as well as with the separation of human beings into those who are granted human dignity and basic rights, and those who are not given a fair chance. Making claims to power with the resources appropriate for today means persuading and generating confidence that the strategy is really directed at the goal of developing a cultural society in which all people can participate in the processes of exchange, and can preserve their identity in groups, ethnicities, religious communities, regions and nations.

Anyone who tolerates or supports a policy of power that is quite clearly not aimed at this demand is ultimately complicit in the increase in global differences and the fact that the globalisation game is associated with the increased risk of disaster. Anyone who shuts his eyes to acts of blackmail, exploitation, oppression or human rights abuses, barbaric practices or the pressure to remain silent, that are carried out by a state, a caste, a group, a mafia-like organisation, may have different motives for this. One of these is fear and the legitimate consideration that the safety of one's own family is more important than social relationships characterised by fairness. However, anyone who has a real possibility to do something against this – on the basis of humanity and non-violence – and even if this is still a very weak impetus, is missing the opportunity to contribute to making the world a better place.

When considering the relevant decisions it must be clear that players who use positions of power in a way that does not satisfy the demands of humanity place themselves ethically and morally at a very low level. There is no reason for the suspicion that they are entitled to a remarkable degree of reputation. This rule applies irrespective of property, wealth, the potential for physical threat, historical justification or merits acquired in the past.

There is a particular problem in achieving the not at all utopian vision of a fair world, that each people and each state can of course only choose a path in a sovereign way, based on internal processes of decision-making. In principle the global community has no entitlement to a dirigiste intervention from outside. However, as part of the informational and economic processes of exchange it must try to assert humanist demands. But a clever approach requires that this is preferably done in the form of offers that could appear acceptable as part of the cultural identity of the particular country, rather than through pressure, a threatening position and the acquisition of land and resources.

5.6 *Short-sightedness of democracy and the professionalism trap*

In section 1.9 the case was made that the short-sightedness of democracy is an important reason why society consistently largely fails when striving to eliminate its dramatic deficiencies. In section 4.2 it was suggested that the professionalism trap is one of the reasons why there is a constant risk of the erosion of political pluralism and democracy (risk 2). The most important of the problems to be mentioned in this regard are as follows:

- Short legislative periods are a factor that significantly limit the ability of the legislative to make decisions that are important in the long-term, but which tend to be related to unpleasant cuts in the nearer future.
- Politicians are partly dependent on using the expertise of lobbyists, as well as paying heed to the mood that prevails in this particularly influential section of the electorate. As far as the lobbyists are concerned it is legitimate that they represent the views of their particular interest groups in a professional way.
- Research and development projects are mainly given resources that are invested in these projects strategically by financially strong interest groups.

- In many democracies, the balance in the systematic and fair organisation of society is increasingly affected by corruption and crime.
- In other state systems, in which important democratic rights or human rights are not important, there is even less expectation that they will make a contribution to developing human society that would be characterised by fairness, far-sightedness or conscientiousness.
- Again, one can clearly not expect that advanced democracies will at all times behave fairly towards less affluent people or societies that have different world views.
- Crises which, not least, go back to systematic deficiencies in politics and in the value system also lead to pressure for action, where there is limited scope for a fair and strategically cleverly applied policy. Quotations from the political debate such as "We must solve the problems gradually" or "We will proceed cautiously" illustrate very well the level at which political action often takes place.

These characteristics of democratic political events could be denounced, demonised, cursed – they must, at least, be the subject of fierce debate. In fact, there are good reasons why the democratic process exhibits these tendencies. The price of a policy where everyone can participate and where mandates regularly expire and are reassigned is that there is no authority that is active in terms of planning for a longer period, and that systematically guides destinies. Instead, each step must continually be the result of considering all interests. Other approaches – such as for example that of a planned economy or the most diverse forms of dictatorship – have shown the fatal consequences that can arise if the state removes itself too far from the principle of the separation of powers.

On the other hand, it is not plausible to expect an individual to control his needs, his intellect and his way of life, and for him to learn to act methodically, if we may not make this demand on the mankind organism. What is the cause for this contradiction? What is really wrong here?

This contradiction arises less from the fact that the division of the democratic process into three powers, legislative, executive and judiciary, is wrong, but from the fact that a fourth component is needed, but that this is too poorly developed. This is the ability of democratic society, not only to direct its decisions in relation to the acute pressure of the fluctuating moods and balances of power, but also at the same time to include elements that embody analytical and planning approaches. This involves the ability of democratic society to submit to the legislative analyses, hypotheses and plans on the subject of the methodical development of democratic society that could really satisfy the global dimension of the mankind dilemma and might be able to gain a majority of votes. It is the ability of society to lead an open and positive discourse on its own future and to develop feasible strategic solutions. In this regard, if one looks at this in a very abbreviated form, then on the plus side this includes, inter alia, the following points:

- In large parts of the world there is a pronounced media culture that can develop on the basis of the right to freedom of expression.
- In many countries there are protest movements that form to combat social or political problems.

- There are many organisations, educational establishments, academic communities and think tanks in the world that discuss sociological, ecological, social, economic and political problems and other issues. In fact, many of these institutions are relatively close to interest groups, lobbying expertise and to the professionalism trap through their funding bodies or through a specified range of issues. On the other hand a reasonably successful discussion about the issues of our time is no longer possible without a largely open-ended and constructive approach.
- The global communication process that takes place on the Internet is, inter alia, also characterised by discussions in which political issues are addressed.

On the debit side, however, the following should be mentioned,

- that, with regard to social processes and the question of how these can be assessed and influenced, there is also something like the sovereignty of interpretation that is hotly disputed in terms of ensuring claims to power using professional means. In this respect, today the world is still too much under the spell of two prominent historical factors. These are, first, the failure of left ideologies and second, the great significance of the Chicago neoliberal school.
- The former has led to the fact that today it is positively frowned upon to reflect ideological perceptions that are primarily committed to fairness.
- The latter has filled the gap that has resulted from this by the declared principle of self-interest, greed, the maximisation of shareholder value, privatisation as a global strategy for solving problems and the fairy tale of the market as a law of nature etc. been

assigned a place in the global value system that allows ethical standards to be too much on the margins.

Today it is largely undisputed that neoliberalism is an aberration and that there should be more regulation once again. This need had already resulted from the crises that have been observed since 2008.

Moreover, it would however be sensible to accept the fact that society does not have enough sustainable ideological hypotheses and strategies to solve problems that could better satisfy both the global dimension as well as ethical demands. In relation to the sovereignty of interpretation, it should be noted that this is only given collectively to the sovereign holder of authority, i.e. the people or all human beings.

Fortunately the media culture is so well developed, at least in part, that the ethical deficiencies of global power poker are also constantly severely criticised and so these can generally be exposed as such. However, it seems to be slightly more difficult to open up new prospects that would strengthen the hope that there could possibly be effective approaches to solutions to some of the antagonisms.

The protest movements provide reason to hope that civil society is able to fight injustice and grievances by taking risks. At the same time it often appears very difficult to take useful action and to achieve tangible progress.

The educational and academic community, institutes and think tanks, organisations and foundations make many valuable contributions to the sociopolitical discourse, without which today's world would be much more hopeless. But the overall balance still seems a little too restrained. The approach could be more imaginative, less respectful towards social conventions, as well as slightly more directed to global affluence than too much to the focus that is suggested in each case.

Again, in the Internet there is no shortage of the necessary disrespect. Every day the net is inundated with heretical blogs on every possible subject. However, overall narcissisms and the destructive troll culture play a prominent role here. There are also attempts to discuss social problems more seriously, but generally these meet with no real response. This is still most successful in relation to protest movements.

We could talk about a discourse on the methodical development of global civilisation if it were possible to bring together positive aspects from all these processes as much as possible. This process could then be justifiably described as "open" if it features at least the following characteristics:

- Respect, in this sense: that particular historical situations are regarded as the result of constructive efforts by all human beings who have ever been born; respect in the sense that it is not sensible simply to ignore or to brush aside previous experiences and knowledge.
- Disrespect in this sense: that no dogma will be accepted, that theories, conventions and value systems will be scrutinised unconditionally, that inputs from elites and professional participants are not treated any differently than that of other participants, that suggestions that come from economic or military powers are not accepted.
- Communication is carried out in an environment that is characterised by constructiveness and inventiveness. Schools and ideologies that regularly produce

knee-jerk defensive reactions or continued trench warfare are not suited to play a role in this discourse. If there is doubt, a new language must be found for the respective topics.

- A primary focus on the main priorities for global society, where of course the basis is an image of human beings and society that respects individuality, diversity and cultural identities.
- There should be no fear of large international groups, the most powerful states, important oligopolies, criminal organisations. If the global social discourse avoids the really big questions and players, then it can be ignored. It may be necessary for people who are particularly exposed here to be protected by global democratic legitimisation and by a global executive.
- The discourse occurs at an international level. In principle, it is open to all human beings. The discourse takes place in the universal language – de facto this is English. With regard to opinion-forming processes that are carried out on the Internet, it is recommended that secure identities should be required for those taking part.
- An important aim is to produce analysis, hypotheses and strategic concepts that can be provided as a model to the legislative powers, and that can assist them to make decisions which, if necessary, also involve unpleasant measures, or which carry particular risks. The previous open discussion to a certain extent ensures that people are not surprised by the consequences.
- The discourse is characterised by the fact that it can, at least partly, involve inputs that may seem naive.

Another characteristic is that participation is possible generally and at any time without the need to spend large amounts of money or effort.

- However, the method of operating is in principle also directed at science and professionalism. In this case, professionalism is meant in the sense of real substance and solidity, not in the sense of being dazzled by a beautiful or populist facade. Furthermore, professionalism is meant in the sense of the greatest possible independence or the greatest possible proximity to human beings as a whole, not in the sense of proximity to any other kind of sponsor or authority, or not in the sense of proximity to the professionalism trap.
- The discourse never leads to a final result. It is certainly scarcely possible to retain or develop a certain level of inventiveness, once this has been achieved. But it would not be very helpful if one were to be thus seduced into dogmas or ideologies.

This book can be understood as a contribution to this discourse.

5.7 The road to the cultural society

How can human society finally manage to take the road towards culture, for it to seriously seek the well-being of all its members and skilfully avoid allowing bad things to happen?

Quite simply: the world develops as its citizens want it to develop.

History shows us how society is inclined to learn lessons. For example, it took the Second World War for the UN to be founded in 1945 and for the "Universal Declaration of Human Rights" to be proclaimed on December 10th 1948. It also apparently took this terrible disaster for the attitude of significant parts of society towards the problem of hunger to no longer be determined by Malthus' inhuman "Essay on the Principle of Population", but by international norms and by the desire to establish social justice that, inter alia, led in 1945 to the foundation of the FAO (Food and Agriculture Organization; cf. Ziegler 2013, 66ff.).

If we extrapolate this ability to acquire knowledge, which is clearly stupid, then this will certainly result in far-reaching events and in even significantly worse irreparable damage than has already occurred today, before it is possible to actually, inevitably, turn things around.

If we return to the mode of operation of the human brain there are, in general terms, two ways in which the human being can acquire knowledge. The way that, for example, is already available, at least for mammals, is that of learning by experience, also called "trial and error". In this case there must first be significant changes, something must go wrong, there must be some harm, there must be an accident before there is a learning effect. The second way is that of fantasy. In this case it is enough if hypotheses are used via the ability for simulation and recombination in the world of the imagination or in Popper's World 3, that the possible consequences of action are considered, with the help of the AA, to verify these and to draw the necessary conclusions. In short: reason is used.

In principle it is not a problem for individual humans. It is the rule that sensible decisions are taken before harm occurs. At the level of society as a whole, this seems to be considerably more difficult. Here it apparently regularly requires a major accident, a terrible war, an environmental disaster, a terrorist attack, the regional expansion of a criminal or Mafia-like cancer or similar disastrous incidents. Climbing the pyramid of needs in society as a whole is marked by constant cases of destruction.

The crucial problem here is the focus on thinking and the power arrows that work as part of the social power system. Assuming that a large number of human beings would be worried, through the actions of society as a whole and the global context, they would have access to sufficient information and the will to use this, so it would be possible for political movements to emerge, each with sufficient potential for a timely submission. However, this is not the case. A large number of human beings are much more inclined to focus on more obvious themes or on a belief, to leave well alone and not to deliberately use the natural mandate to organise the cultural society. The inclination towards belief, whether this is a religious or an atheistic belief (e. g. that of the free market, democracy, science), is not the problem here. Belief is much more a necessity, as already explained above. The problem first exists if belief tempts one into not noticing the natural mandate and not using the self-conscious mind for this, depending on the opportunities available to affect the development of society as a whole and thus one's own future, and the well-being of genetic and spiritual descendants.

Only when a decisive majority of human beings have an attitude that includes dealing with the natural mandate in a purposeful manner, then the chances of avoiding disaster and in favour of continuing to develop the cultural society are good. For this to happen it is definitely not enough to hope for the emergence of democratic relationships and, if they do occur, for them to act as a model and then, after voting, to assume that everything that could have been done has been done. Of course, the democratic form of representative participation is one of the most important and basic requirements of a humanist society. But participating in this process as a voter is not everything. For the demand to result in human reason in society, this form of influence is ultimately only a particularly comfortable solution for a small part of the range of problems.

Appreciating the natural mandate means much more than going to vote. In general it means being critical of all processes on a daily basis, whether as an employee, a boss, the owner of a firm, a shareholder, a proprietor, a civil servant, a politician, a citizen, an aesthete, a consumer, a market participant, a scientist, a member of an organisation, an activist etc. In all spheres of society the creative influence of any participant in the social exchange processes, sustained by the self-conscious mind, counts.

As mentioned, it is down to every individual human being but those who already live in cultural affluence or those who have even acquired an influential position in society are given a particularly prominent role.

In each case it should be considered that the tools are simply too big today, the means too powerful to leave it to a strategy of trial and error, or to give in to fatalism. The powerful means of our time would not have been developed from fatalistic attitudes, so it can only be wrong to give in to this.

One of the future scenarios could involve a window of opportunity for mankind so as to make serious adjustments to the demands of the time, and to be able to pursue the road to a global culture and an affluent society. If it misses this window of opportunity, a situation of self-reinforcing global destruction could occur that may noticeably put the last world war into perspective. Hence it is necessary not to underestimate the impending shortage of resources and the environmental risks, as well as – depending on the personal situation – to find one's way out of the vicious circle of hate, religious blindness or the comfortable niche of affluence, and to achieve a consensus based on respect for fellow human beings and in terms of nature. If this project does not happen for lack of participation there are no grounds for optimism.

Two points are still particularly important. The first is the continued willingness of those participating to give something up. As plausible as it seems for human beings to demand to hang onto the precious hate or affluence, it is also wrong. One can only gain something new if one is willing to give something up, and without any guarantees. Second, politics must be understood as a strategic design problem. Politicians who do not make this the focus of their action, but who instead serve short-sighted client interests, and voters who expect this from politicians, have deserved any disastrous scenario that occurs.

It is a question of whether the mankind child still has to always touch every hotplate before he or she understands that it is not a good idea to do this. This has already been avoided at least twice – there was no nuclear war in the Cuban missile crisis and on 26.09.1983 (cf. Hannusch 2012), if only because there was a lot of good fortune. What counts, however, is the fact that at that time war did not escalate beyond the so-called cold war phase.

The current situation is much less clear-cut. If one wanted to, one could easily argue about the right strategy and about the sense and nonsense of special decisions. The understanding that is needed at the level of society as a whole is much higher in the current state of affairs than in the Cold War. Above all, there also seems to be no clear evidence about when exactly the deadlines for necessary decisions expire. However, many deadlines have long been exceeded – it is certain that many kinds of animal and plant have been decimated or even made extinct, that the use of modern weapons and nuclear accidents have claimed countless lives etc. The question is: How far do we want to go?

Appendix

The self-conscious mind

In particular, Popper/Eccles 2006 also ask the question of how the self-conscious mind is achieved and where it is located. In this book, the question is answered in a slightly different way from Popper and Eccles. Some of the aspects of the different interpretations are discussed below.

The book "The Self and Its Brain" discusses the question of what the self-conscious human mind is, what it represents, in what it consists, and where it is located. The book approaches this question from the philosophical (Karl R. Popper, 1–224) and from the neurological aspect (John C. Eccles, 225–421).

Amongst other things, Popper's contribution is characterised by the premise that, in relation to the body-mind problem, a differentiation should be made between three worlds. Quotation (16f.): "It may be useful, for various reasons, […] to arrange some of these cosmic evolutionary stages in the following Table 1. […] It has the […] advantage of summing up very briefly what seem to be some of the greatest events of creative evolution or of emergent evolution." (See table 3, taken from Popper/Eccles 2006, 16)

Eccles refers to these descriptions and adds a more sophisticated examination related to the results of human behaviour. On the one hand he sees "KNOWLEDGE IN OBJECTIVE SENSE" in World 3 and distinguishes between "Cultural heritage coded on material substrates" and "Theoretical systems". He sees another part of the results of human behaviour in World 1 – these are "ARTEFACTS", respectively "Material substrates of human creativity, of tools, of machines, of books, of works of art, of music". Between World 2, consisting of outer sense, inner sense and ego or self, and World 1, he defines an interface located in the cerebrum, which he calls liaison brain (359f.).

Table 3 – Some Cosmic Evolutionary Stages

World 3 (the products of the human mind)	(6) Works of Art and Science (including Technology) (5) Human Language. Theories of Self and of Death
World 2 (the world of subjective experiences)	(4) Consciousness of Self and Death (3) Sentience (Animal Consciousness)
World 1 (the world of physical objects)	(2) Living Organisms (1) The Heavier Elements; Liquids and Crystals (0) Hydrogen and Helium

How Eccles defines the interdependencies between the three worlds is expressed in pages 359f.:

> "Everything in existence and in experience is subsumed in one or other of three worlds: World 1, the world of physical objects and states; World 2, the world of states of consciousness and subjective knowledge of all kinds; World 3, the world of man-made culture, comprising the whole of objective knowledge. […] Furthermore it is proposed that there is interaction between these worlds. There is reciprocal interaction be-

tween Worlds 1 and 2, and between Worlds 2 and 3 generally […] via the mediation of World 1. When the objective knowledge of World 3 (the man-made world of culture) is encoded on various objects of World 1 – books, pictures, structures, machines –, it can be consciously perceived only when projected to the brain by the appropriate receptor organs and afferent pathways. Reciprocally the World 2 of conscious experience can bring about changes in World 1, in the first place in the brain, then in muscular contractions, World 2 in that way being able to act extensively on World 1. This is the postulated operation in voluntary movement that has been considered in chapter E3. We may formulate the conjectured interactions of the trialist-interactionist hypothesis as: World 1 ↔ World 2 and World 3 ↔ World 1 ↔ World 2, where World 2 → World 1 contains the problem of voluntary action (chapter E3) and World 1 → World 2 the problem of conscious perception (chapter E2). However, when the self-conscious mind is engaged in creative thinking on problems or ideas, there would seem to be a direct interaction of World 2 and World 3 […]."

In subchapter 42 "The Self Anchored in World 3", Popper states: "But the human consciousness of self transcends, I suggest, all purely biological thought." (144) And below: "In all these matters it is the anchorage of the self in World 3 that makes the difference. The basis of it is human language which makes it possible for us to be not only subjects, centres of action, but also objects of our own critical thought, of our own critical judgement." (144)

In this respect, Popper's approach can be welcomed. In relation to Darwin's theory of evolution, this comment can also be regarded as quite helpful (Chapter P6 “Summary”, 209f.):

> “(9) Natural selection, and selection pressure, are usually thought of as the results of a more or less violent struggle for life.
>
> But with the emergence of mind, of World 3, and of theories, this changes. We may let our theories fight it out – we may let our theories die in our stead.”

From this perspective, it is very reassuring that human evolution is in fact closely related to the development of consciousness, and that the struggle for life may take place essentially in linguistic and mental spheres.

According to this, J. C. Eccles develops a dualist-interactionist hypothesis on consciousness. (“Preface”, 226): “According to the dualist-interactionist philosophy presented in this book, the brain is a machine of almost infinite complexity and subtlety, and in special regions, under appropriate conditions, it is open to interaction with World 2, the world of conscious experience.” This statement makes clear that Eccles assigns an essential part of the brain to World 1, probably comprising at least the complete sensorimotor part of the neural system, supporting perception and coordinated action.

A further interesting statement is provided e.g. in subchapter 50 “The Self-conscious Mind and the Brain” (359): “It is proposed that superimposed upon the neural machinery in all its performance, as outlined in chapters E1, E2, E3, E4, E5 and E6 – there are at certain sites of the cerebral hemisphere (the liaison areas) effective interactions with the self-conscious mind, both in receiving and in giving.”

This is explained in more detail in subchapter 51 (362):

> “A brief initial outline of the hypothesis may be stated

as follows. The self-conscious mind is actively engaged in reading out from the multitude of active centres at the highest level of brain activity, namely the liaison areas of the dominant cerebral hemisphere. The self-conscious mind selects from these centres according to attention, and from moment to moment integrates its selection to give unity even to the most transient experiences. Furthermore the self-conscious mind acts upon these neural centres modifying the dynamic spatiotemporal patterns of the neural events. Thus we propose that the self-conscious mind exercises a superior interpretative and controlling role upon the neural events."

In the rest of Chapter E7 it is explained that there are cortical modules in the liaison centres that are contact points of the physical world (World 1) to the self-conscious mind (World 2). These contact points are not always open for interaction with consciousness, but there is a constantly changing pattern of open and closed modules in which, with modules that are not accessible in this process, as well as with neural sections that are further away, interactions are indirectly possible via the open modules.

The following sentence in the "Summary" of the section by J. C. Eccles (374) can be accepted: "It can be claimed that the strong dualist-interactionist hypothesis that has been here developed has the recommendation of its great explanatory power." In particular, the assumption that consciousness is something that has a distinctive life of its own and that reciprocal, bidirectional, interactional processes take place between the self-conscious mind and other neural processes, and thereby also the physiological and physical world (World 1), should also be accepted.

Furthermore, however, there is a conclusion that should be questioned here (376): "But the question: where is the self-conscious mind located? is unanswerable in principle. This can be appreciated when we consider some components of the self-conscious mind. It makes no sense to ask where are located the feelings of love or hate, or of joy or fear, or of such values as truth, goodness and beauty which apply to mental appraisals."

This assumption is here opposed by the following postulate:

The self-conscious mind can only be located in the brain – and especially in those centres that Eccles described as the liaison brain (subchapter 52, 444): "As a consequence of the investigations (chapters E5, E6) on global and circumscribed lesions of the human brain we may conjecture that the liaison brain comprises a large part of the dominant hemisphere, particularly the linguistic areas and the polymodal areas as well as a large area of the prefrontal lobe". But while, in these areas of the brain, Eccles only sees the contact points to the self-conscious mind, it should be asserted here that they are also at the same time the residence of the self-conscious mind.

At the same time it should once again be emphasised that the self-conscious mind is independent, autonomous; it should not be equated with the world of other neural processes (and therefore World 1), but it stands with it in an interactional inter-relationship. How is that compatible? A possible, apparently plausible explanation for this is as follows:

In principle the processes in the cerebrum flow in two modes – first in an operative mode and second in a simulation mode. The operative mode is responsible for tasks in which interactions with the environment actually take place, for example when solving a card-sorting exercise, when reading a text, when speaking etc., and of course in all physical activities (work, sport). The simulation mode is active in brain processes that are not directly connected to such external interactions. In this case, similar processes occur as in the operative mode, but the efferent transmission is blocked and no real afferent processes are involved, instead the neural processes are supplied by recollection or memory.

The thesis of the simulation mode is almost obligatory if one considers that impulse control is an essential characteristic of human behaviour. Furthermore, this thesis is supported by the knowledge that, during thought processes, there is in part latent control of muscles and activity patterns.

The operative mode and the simulation mode always flow simultaneously in the human brain and they (in part) use the same areas of the brain. The neural processes of both modes can here be regarded as independent, that is to say, they are not identical and they are also not directly related, but they are in an interactive relationship. The criticism of epiphenomenalism and parallelism in Popper (see Chapter P3, subchapters 20, 24) should also be fully satisfied here.

The question of how the contact points between World 1 and World 2 that are open in a particular moment are explainable can be answered by saying that it is the intersection of the modules that is used by the operative and, at the same time, the simultaneously operating simulation mode, or is activated by it. Apart from that, the interaction between World 1 and 2 occurs through the memory.

On the question of feelings and emotions, an explicit explanation should also be provided in this context. The following conclusion by Eccles should not only be regarded as unsatisfactory, but also as unnecessary (see also quotation above): "It makes no sense to ask where are located the feelings of love or hate, or of joy or fear, or of such values as truth, goodness and beauty which apply to mental appraisals." (376) Because elsewhere in Eccles the answer to the question of where emotions have their origin is provided (see Chapter E2, subchapter 13: "Emotional Colouring of Conscious Perceptions", 273):

> "Nauta [1971] conjectures that the state of the organism's internal milieu (hunger, thirst, sex, fear, rage, pleasure) is signalled to the prefrontal lobes from the hypothalamus, the septal nuclei and various components of the limbic system such as the hippocampus and the amygdala. [...] Thus, by their projections to the prefrontal lobes, the hypothalamus and the limbic system modify and colour with emotion the conscious perceptions derived from sensory inputs and superimpose on them motivational drives."

From this perspective, at first there is no doubt about how externally supplied perceptions and the perceptions of physical activities and vegetative processes are enriched by emotions. But how do feelings which are linked to higher values like "truth, goodness and beauty" and the further endless variety of human sensations, now develop? The answer that should be given here is: in the simulation mode emotions, together with sensory (more precisely: sensorimotor) incidents, are primarily supplied from the capacity to remember, that includes the emotions. In neuronal information processing in this mode, new informational constructs of almost any extent develop in which generally emotions are involved. From these processes inevitably new, synthetic emotions must develop, which would never occur without the conscious part of neuronal information processing. This is how typically human feelings and higher values (in the positive and in the negative sense) develop. Generally it can be said here that any emotions always express the relevance that the informational constructs, to which they are connected, have for the person in whose brain they originate. Unlike in a computer, all information is therefore coloured by an emotional component in this way – this is what is human in neuronal information processing.

The emotional components can vary in strength – from extreme, overwhelming power, up to an almost complete lack of emotion. The fact that practically all processes in the brain are in this way provided to a greater or lesser extent with meaningful, constructive, prioritising components is the essential and probably extremely beneficial difference to the computer.

In the chapter about the conscious memory (E8, 377ff.) a close relationship is established between the self-conscious mind and memory, and especially with short-term memory. Two limbic circuits are described (subchapter 62, 394ff.), whose fundamental accomplishments are attributed to short-term memory and long-term memory. Neural activities take place in these circuits, in which spatial-temporal neural patterns are continually repeated and modified. A decisive role is played here by attention control, that is again closely connected to the self-conscious mind.

In subchapter 60: "The Role of the Self-Conscious Mind in Short-Term Memory" it is stated (387f.):

“Let us consider some simple and unique perceptual experience, for example the first sight of a bird or flower hitherto unknown to us or of a new model of a car. First, there are the many stages of encoded transmission from retinal image to the various levels of the visual cortex with feature recognition as the highest interpretive level so far recognized, as described in chapter E2. At a further stage we propose the activation of modules of the liaison brain that are ‘open’ to World 2 (chapter E7), the consequent read-out by the self-conscious mind giving the perceptual experience with all its sensual richness. This read-out by the self-conscious mind involves the integration into a unified experience of the specific activities of many modules, an integration that gives the pictured uniqueness to the experience (chapter E7). Furthermore, it is a two-way action, the self-conscious mind modifying the modular activity as well as receiving from it, and possibly evaluating it by testing procedures in an input-output manner. [...] Moreover we have to postulate closed self-reexciting chains in these ongoing patterns of modular interaction. [...]

As long as the modular activities continue in this specific patterned interaction, we assume that the self-conscious mind is continuously able to read it out according to its interests and its attention. [...] We propose that the continued activity of the modules can be secured by continuous active intervention or reinforcement by the self-conscious mind, which in this way can hold memories by processes that we experience and refer to as either verbal or non-verbal (pictorial or musical, for example) rehearsal. As soon as the self-conscious mind engages in some other task, this reinforcement ceases, that specific pattern of neuronal activities subsides and the short-term memory is lost."

The duration and number of repetitions of particular activities in the short-term memory circuit again has a substantial influence on whether and how certain patterns are also entered in the long-term memory as chemical changes in synapses. Furthermore, here the strength of the emotions involved plays an important role.

In relation to the activity control circuit of the short-term memory, the role of the area of the brain called the hippocampus is particularly accentuated. Without the accomplishments of this area it is possible to retain particular patterns and therefore the memory content of the short-term memory, as long as attention is completely focused on this, or as long as no other activity patterns appear. With the involvement of the hippocampus, however, it is possible to get patterns circulating once again, even after attention has been impaired. In a way, this area of the brain represents the difference between single-threading and multi-threading – if one wants to express it in the language of computer science. It is thus possible to simultaneously execute several perception and activity programmes.

As already mentioned above, the hypothesis that the self-conscious mind interacts with the rest of the nervous system via the liaison brain, but can itself not be located, shall be rejected here. It is much more the case that it is precisely the limbic circuits that, particularly in relation to the ability to switch attention back and forth between the different patterns, also constitute the self-conscious mind. It is claimed that, on the one hand, perception and activity programmes constantly flow simultaneously towards direct interaction with the environment, and, on the other hand, that this is also true of simulation programmes, which represent the self-conscious mind and short-term memory. Here all threads are independent processes, on the one hand, but parts of the patterns can also be bypassed at the same time. It should once again be emphasised that it is assumed that the thought processes, that is, the processes that flow in the simulation mode or that represent the self-conscious mind, directed through the limbic circuits, flow precisely in the same areas of the brain that are also responsible for the accomplishments of language and coordinated interaction. In parallel to this, these areas of the brain can, almost simultaneously, be used for real interactions with the environment, without both being necessarily closely connected to each other.

Of course it is obvious that during a physical activity the mind also turns towards a suitable topic, but this is not inevitably the case. Instead it is possible that the mind, for example, is occupied with planning a journey, while another part of the nervous system (another thread) is engaged in perception and control tasks when working in the garden. After a telephone call in which a family matter is discussed and an appointment is noted, both programmes can again be assimilated.

It is just as plausible that the ability to multitask must have limits – in particular, if maximum performance is demanded from the same area of the brain. For example, it seems rather difficult to reconcile making a speech on an intellectually challenging subject, while at the same time thinking about a completely different, no less complex subject. On its own, the former demand is complex enough, as it already requires simultaneous processes in the speech area – on the one hand for speech itself and on the other for reviewing the meaning of what should be said and for planning the next few sentences.

The simultaneous hypothesis makes the assertion that the residence of the self-conscious mind is to be attributed to areas of the brain that also, simultaneously, perform important functions in the interaction with World 1 and which, if you like, form the liaison brain, compatible with the demand to maintain the dualist-interactionist perception in the philosophical dimension of the mind-body problem. Here there should be no definite assertions that there are not also, in part, modules and areas that no longer fulfil World 1 tasks – that may rather be the subject for further research. But it shall be established that this kind of area does not necessarily have to exist and that consciousness, as it were, is not required to have its own, dedicated residence but that, with the simulation mode, the basis for a self-conscious, independent mind is already fulfilled.

On the philosophical side the question of who, possibly, is right or wrong, of materialism, behaviourism, identity theory, epiphenomenalism, Descartes, Newton, Leibnitz, another school or Popper, will not be discussed here. Popper's philosophical explanations, as well as the claim to take a dualist-interactionist position, are accepted in a rather provisional way, and the search is merely for a new, seemingly plausible answer to the question of the residence of the self-conscious mind. Again, this does not come about because of an academic interest, but because it is of crucial importance for the question of balanced relations in the human organism and in the mankind organism. This is particularly about the assumption that the neurological processes relating to World 1 and World 2 – even though they are also independent processes that represent a duality – fully share the mechanism through which emotions and feelings are involved, however. In both cases the emotions come from the same primary source (see above Popper/Eccles 2006, 273). The difference is that, in direct relation to sensory perceptions and motor activities (World 1), these are primary physiologically-induced feelings, while with memory content, it is about remembered feelings that, in relation to the self-conscious mind and the simulatory-synthetic neural patterns generated by this (World 2), are again enriched by related synthetic combinations of feelings.

In each case, feelings and emotions represent the relevance that a neural process – of whatever kind – has for people in which this process occurs. All processes that penetrate consciousness (probably also those that do not penetrate consciousness), have such a relevance component. These can, certainly, be stronger or weaker, but without these no consciousness is possible. In fact it is a fundamental law that all neural processes are implicitly subject to constant assessment. This also occurs with any synthetic informational constructs via the same mechanism as in purely operative (World 1) processes via limbic circuits.

The self-conscious mind is kept going, modulated and directed by the limbic circuit. However, it consists of all the brain processes that take place in the perception mechanism, the control mechanism and in the memory. Therefore it is realised as a process of inner experience, that takes place in the entirety of all neural projection spaces. Also of quite crucial importance here is the fact that this inner experience continues incessantly while awake, so that the illusion of total consciousness develops that is integrated along the timeline. This total consciousness must therefore be described as an illusion, because the processes that have already escaped from the short-term memory still only haunt this as scraps of memories that can, however, be used at any time as reference points to recall detailed memories.

Why does a computer strongly and always tend towards absurd reactions that one must laboriously expel (e.g. by tests), and why does the human being typically not tend towards these? Because any processing of information in humans is always subject to assessment, because absurd answers and reactions are immediately and directly exposed through some kind of bad feeling, and because the limbic circuits automatically look for answers that convey a sufficiently positive feeling.

The universality of the world of emotions, the statement that here there is a continuity, a coherent natural law that is valid from the lower to the higher neural processes, provides a useful link from philosophy and neurology to the humanistic psychology of A. Maslow and Maslow's pyramid of needs.

Glossary

AA/Attention Assessor – Central controller of the cerebrum, which combines activity and attention control with the emotional evaluation of the neural patterns. In the → operational mode of the neural system, the AA controls processes of perception and coordinated action. However, processes of remembering, → recombination, thinking are controlled in the → simulation mode. The assessment or evaluation of the neural pattern occurs in both modes, in the sense of their choice and modulation (attention, attentiveness, coordination of activities), and in the sense of the evaluation of their positive or negative effect on the organism (emotion). The system, which is described here as AA, correlates with achievements which, in the literature, are described on the one hand as short-term memory and on the other as attentional control. The signals circulating in this system, and which are subject to emotional evaluation, are also responsible for inscribing the neural patterns in the long-term memory. The AA is probably mainly located in central brain areas, such as the limbic system, the hippocampus etc., as well as in the prefrontal cortex. In addition, the vegetative centre of the cerebrum, called the hypothalamus, should play a decisive role, through which the control processes described as homeostasis, to maintain the essential natural substance balance, come about. While in the → operational mode, activities to satisfy basic needs are controlled by the AA, evaluation components are integrated into the brain processes via this vegetative interface. In this way basic experiences are stored in the long-term memory from which, with other brain activities controlled by the AA, all the more complex forms of experiences, the contents of consciousness and emotions arise.

AA/differential working principle of the AA – As in a closed control loop, the primary principle of the AA is to ensure the compensation of randomly occurring deviations between actual and nominal values. The scale of the homeostatic signals and feelings of pain which affect the AA can normally only range from extreme deprivation (close to minus infinity), to complete tranquillity (close to zero). However, after removal of the greatest need, the experience of deprivation automatically provokes the pursuit of the opposite (in the direction plus infinity). The neural system, and above all the AA, automatically act in a precautionary way, and the indicator for this is feelings which can express the opposite of perceptions of deprivation. From this principle flows intra-neural competition for signal sequences, which can represent the highest possible level of vitality. Thus the differential scale of human perceptions ranges from extreme frustrations and anxieties, to elation and aesthetic experiences. Without regular amplitudes in feelings in a positive and negative direction, and without any corresponding tensions, any stimulus would cease.

Aesthetics Principle – More precisely: **Principle of differential aesthetics**. Summarises the world of human perceptions and feelings as a unit and recognises it as a matter of (aesthetic) evaluation. Excitation patterns and memory contents in the cerebrum are fundamentally and generally attached to the principle of emotion. Homeostasis, lower and higher needs, form a unit insofar as they build on each other. Basic experiences develop from lower needs and their satisfaction, from which, through → simulation and

→ recombination, more complex contents and emotions arise, which again correlate to higher needs. In this sense, both the emotional sphere of the human psyche and the system of needs form a unit. To characterise this unit, the term "Principle of differential aesthetics" is suggested because it considers all the abysses of being, but, at the same time, the optimistic and constructive statement that a life is achievable that is characterised by the pursuit of the highest feelings and their partial fulfilment. Ultimately this approach is also plausible because aesthetic accents (such as, for example, attending a classical concert) logically lead to the satisfaction of basic needs also being celebrated in aesthetic circumstances (e. g. a restaurant visit after the concert). Here it is important to understand that fine aesthetics (in the artistic or etiquette sense), are probably not the highest form of aesthetics, but that the latter can only develop if it is made possible for the existing hedonistic-narcissistic shadows, or a limited horizon, to be overcome. The result of the differential functioning of the → AA is that, for example, a sporting activity with the thrill of a certain risk can impart a more intensive aesthetic experience than a comparatively uniform sport. However, there is the suspicion that here no important shadows are overcome. Fulfilment is achieved much more if, for example, one provides support to deprived people in some form. According to the differential principle, this should in particular indicate that the real misery in the world is being fought. The less eyes are closed to the most disgusting excesses of human civilisation, the higher the benefit that the observer may possibly achieve for his mental or aesthetic well-being. If one considers the → mankind organism, the principle of differential aesthetics can also be regarded as generalised insofar as it considers all humans to be aesthetically sentient beings. Another facet of the Aesthetics Principle arises from the comparison of the internal, emotional-aesthetic aspect of the world of human needs, with their external, material aspect. The preconditions for satisfying needs are established on the material side, but their eventual fulfilment always occurs in the emotional-aesthetic sphere. Building on the explanations above, it will be claimed here that aesthetics is the universal and highest fulfilment principle of the neural system, by incorporating the whole of the internal world of the individual and his/her external relationships.

Awfulness effect – Feelings which arise if aesthetic or ethical demands encounter a reality which is formed comparatively crudely or brutally. The → subtlety trend is associated with the demand that humans who sustain this trend find opportunities to manage a more or less blatant contradiction between a high cultural demand and an "awful" reality. For this, a correspondingly large capacity for suffering, as well as an explanatory model, are required, which sustains the hope for better times.

Culture Principle – Transfer of the → Aesthetics Principle to society with the rationale that culture is nothing more than the fulfilment of aesthetic demands in society.

Destructiveness case – Occurs if important components of a → vitality system erode, so that synergies are lost and the result is the collapse of parts of the system. This concerns complex phenomena. Examples are conflicts of all kinds, divorces, wars, economic crises, stock exchange crashes as well as, if possible, at least some of the cases of unexpected mental illnesses. There can be identifiable causes for corresponding collapses – such as, for example, an increase in resource shortages. Equally, though, they can result from the natural dynamic of interactions, if, by chance, these lead to a fatal domino effect.

Mankind organism – This term is used to emphasise that all human beings are at the mercy of one another due to manifold interexchange relationships and interdependencies, with the consequence being a common system.

Mental descendants – The human being also always has descendants, even if he does not have children of his own. Through his existence, through any kind of communication, the human being leaves traces in society and thus also in subsequent generations.

Natural mandate – This expresses the fact that every human, simply by being there and living in society, automatically exercises political influence. He can partly pass on this mandate – e. g. as a democratic mandate – but he cannot completely hand this over or avoid this. Furthermore, every interaction in society also results in a creative influence, which can never be fully separated from political influence. If anyone tries not to exercise any political influence, the result is merely that he is thus voting for fatalism or conservativism.

Neurasthenia of economic growth – Neurasthenia of the capitalist economy, its dependence on mood; the constant tendency of the market economy system to crisis; market nervousness; pressure for growth.

Operational mode – Mode of neural processes, in which they control the perception and activity processes, so interactions with the environment.

Professionalism trend – Trend towards the increasing specialisation of the activity profile, and the professionalisation of social processes. Amongst other things it follows that more investment resources and more efficiency are needed in order to achieve comparatively small advances. This trend leads to an increase in the risk that society does indeed excel at increasingly better individual performances, but that in the interdisciplinary field, and in relation to the capacity to manage its destiny sufficiently well, it moves to a fatalistic downward spiral.

Recombination – The recombination or combination of any neural patterns or memory content. It is made possible by the → Attention Assessor in → simulation mode. Another expression for thinking, but it can also better express the fact that this is not always about sophisticated matters, but that there is a continuity of simple anticipatory processes in activity planning and activity control, up to the highest cognitive activities. The basic principle is always the same.

Self-conscious mind – In Popper/Eccles (2006), the self-conscious mind is linked to the so-called World 2, the activities of the short-term memory and the Liaison Brain. The question of where it is located is, however, described as unanswerable. Contrary to this, the self-conscious mind is attributed to the activities of the → Attention Assessor, its mediating function between homeostasis, short-term memory and long-term memory, as well as the thesis of → operational mode and → simulation mode. The question of where the self-conscious mind is located is answered here thus, that the location is the whole of the areas of the brain which are engaged in these processes. These processes enable the human being to go far away mentally from the immediate context of interaction with the environment. The awareness of self results from the possibility of also moving to contexts in which he confronts himself.

Simulation – A model-related simulation of the behaviour of a real system. Usage takes place here, as with the → simulation mode.

Simulation mode – A mode of neural processes, when a generalised inhibitory mechanism in a central area prevents these processes from being directly linked with external perception or activity processes. The brain simulates any excitation patterns and treats the mind and the memory content playfully, without activity or perception processes actually occurring. The complementary principle for this is the → operational mode. The simulatory capabilities of the neural system are closely related to impulse control, → recombination, thinking and → the self-conscious mind. In interaction with memory, → recombination and the → Attention Assessor, the simulation mode facilitates access to neural patterns, which represent information or actions in distant places, in the past, the future or fiction.

Simultaneous – Term for processes that are apparently, but not really executed in parallel (also here applied to the neural system). An example of simultaneous chess: A chess Grand Master plays against 10 opponents, goes from board to board, reflects briefly and each time makes a move; from the viewpoint of the 10 opponents, the Grand Master plays at the same time against all of them. With sufficient capacity of a simultaneously operating system, for the user of the system the difference between real parallelism and simultaneous functions is typically not relevant. Computers mainly operate simultaneously, by multiplexing processes and → threads to small divisions of the processor time. In addition, multiprocessor systems are also able to operate multiple concurrent processes really in parallel.

Subtlety trend – Assumption that a component in the history of human society consists of the fact that, with the passing of time, the fight for existence is relocated to ever more subtle levels. There is, so to speak, a change from barbarism to civilised society, which constantly continues with the build-up of increasingly sophisticated → vitality systems, as long as there is no disruption through increasing resource shortages or through the → destructiveness case. This can also, for example, explain why humans in the affluent society increasingly make mountains out of molehills, and why, from the viewpoint of poorer countries, that could appear ridiculous.

Thread – Is used here in the sense of the concept of threads in IT, which describes particular → simultaneously executed program execution threads. In relation to the human brain, the particular → simultaneously circulating neural patterns in the limbic control system are also brought together with the thread concept.

Vitality system – The whole of physical and mental health, as well as all available mental and economic potential. This concerns all assets, both in the aesthetic and the material sphere, as well as their interrelations. This concept combines the respective components in both spheres and emphasises system identity.

Used both in the sense of the vitality system of the individual and also society. The latter again also combines the vitality systems of the individuals involved, and their interrelations. Finally, the term "social vitality system" is strongly correlated to the concept "human culture", in which, however, the former particularly emphasises the sufficiency aspect. It follows from system identity that it is not simply a question of the accumulation of numerically ascertainable amounts, but that scalar changes in the inputs typically result in discontinuous changes in system parameters. Particularly crucial is the perception that a sufficient vitality system first occurs when a multiplicity of components are established and coordinated. The erosion of fewer components can already lead to the destruction of the system, or to significant restructuring efforts.

Index of illustrations

Index of tables

Bibliography

Conway, Edmund (2012): 50 ideas you really need to know - economics. Quercus, London.

Crouch, Colin (2011): The Strange Non-Death of Neoliberalism. Polity Press, Cambridge (UK) and Malden (USA).

Hannusch, Heidrun (2012): "Der Mann, der die Welt rettete. Raketenalarm in der Sowjetunion. Es droht der Dritte Weltkrieg. Bis Stanislaw Petrow bemerkt, dass es ein Fehlalarm ist." Sächsische Zeitung, 16.11.2012, S. 3.

Hessel, Stéphane (2011): Engagiert Euch! Ullstein Buchverlage, Berlin.

Majetschak, Stefan (2010): Ästhetik zur Einführung. Junius Verlag, Hamburg, 2., unveränderte Auflage.

Maslow, Abraham H. (1987): Motivation and Personality. Third Edition. Addison Wesley Longman, Inc.

Mättig, Thomas (2012): "Kill and go". taz.die tageszeitung, 04.12.2012, S. 12.

Popper, Karl R.; Eccles, John C. (2006): The Self and Its Brain. An Argument for Interactionism. Routledge, London and New York.

Spini, Debora (2006): *La societá civile postnazionale.* Meltemi, Rom.

Stanford, Peter (2010): 50 ideas you really need to know – religion. Quercus, London.

Ziegler, Jean (2011): Der Hass auf den Westen – Wie sich die armen Völker gegen den wirtschaftlichen Weltkrieg wehren. Wilhelm Goldmann Verlag, München, 3. Auflage.

Ziegler, Jean (2013): Betting on Famine. Why the World Still Goes Hungry. The New Press, New York, London.